WINNING AUDITIONS

WINNING AUDITIONS

101 Strategies for Actors

BY MARK BRANDON

Limelight Editions

Published in 2005 by
Limelight Editions (an imprint of Amadeus Press, LLC)
512 Newark Pompton Turnpike
Pompton Plains, New Jersey 07444, USA

For sales, please contact
Limelight Editions
c/o Hal Leonard Corp.
7777 West Bluemound Road
Milwaukee, Wisconsin 53213, USA
Tel. 800-637-2852
Fax 414-774-3259

Website: www.limelighteditions.com

Printed in Canada

Library of Congress Cataloging-in-Publication Data

Brandon, Mark.
  Winning auditions : 101 strategies for actors / Mark
Brandon.— 1st Limelight ed.
    p. cm.
  ISBN 0-87910-316-7 (pbk.)
  1. Acting—Auditions. 2. Acting. I. Title.
PN2071.A92B73 2005
792.02'8'023--dc22

                    2005007654

CONTENTS

CONTENTS

PREFACE

It was an unexpected wake-up call that brought this book to life. For a number of years I'd taught the complexities of acting for the camera. Yet I was dwelling so much on how to effectively *do* the job that I was spending precious little time on how to *get* it. So almost every night, the students in my workshops would stay after class and ask for advice on how to improve their auditions. The good, solid questions of these conscientious actors eventually became my alarm clock.

One evening, in an attempt to address many of these inquiries straightforwardly and all at once, I tried something I'd never done before. I shut off the cameras, put away my clipboard, and gathered everyone around in their chairs. Then I swallowed my teacher's pride and candidly began to describe many of the auditions I had blown as an actor—and there were plenty—whether from poor preparation, mistakes, or just plain ignorance. I finished by explaining what those experiences had taught me and what I had changed in order to do better the next time out.

It wasn't long before everyone else wanted to get involved in the same frank process. The actors jumped in one by one, giving their own personal accounts.

The effect was electric. Everyone took a turn openly sharing experiences that ranged from agonizing setbacks to proud victories. This rewarding development provided a totally unforeseen discovery: one actor's specific difficulties often turned out to be plaguing a number of others as well. And so a lively discussion period took place each evening before class.

These continuing exchanges effectively transformed the nature of my workshop, which became more and more like a group encounter for ardent professionals, each actor unselfishly contributing what he or she had learned in order to benefit the rest. Still, the greatest discovery was yet to come.

This new studio practice seemed so worthwhile and reassuring, I felt compelled to take notes. And I'm very glad I did. Each night, the actors generously offered one another a priceless gift: hard-earned knowledge from the arena of real life. As the notes accumulated, I began to recognize their extraordinary significance: these revelations amounted to nothing less than a bona fide collection of actors' trade secrets.

Looking over this remarkable information, it became obvious that such details were absolutely indispensable for any determined actor. So I finally took all these notes, these "reports from the trenches" as it were, and organized them into a cohesive book format. I hope they will come to serve as a vital resource for all professionals firmly committed to the long haul. So to those actors who got this whole thing started, I remain gratefully indebted. It is to them that this book is dedicated.

As a final note, I've interspersed throughout the book many individual quotations from famous actors. These quotes readily affirm each of these celebrities' own particular philosophies and approaches to this nearly ageless art form. As a result, the reader will doubtless come to appreciate the commonalities that bind all actors; that virtually all performers, great and obscure alike, have shared the same concerns.

Mark Brandon
Vancouver, May 2005

*A heartfelt thanks
to Arran Saul for
his generous assistance
with the original
manuscript.*

INTRODUCTION

As an actor you've picked a very challenging lifestyle, to put it mildly. Through endless round after round of auditions, you have to be completely on your toes, giving 100 percent of everything you've got. Only occasionally will this demanding process be interrupted by your actually landing a part. As a result, it can sometimes begin to seem that the reward doesn't quite equal the enormous amount of work and energy expended to get it.

If you're willing to endure this type of existence—putting up with it year in and year out as nothing but a constant gamble—then you're certainly no hobbyist. You're in the game for good. You're fully aware that what you do remains forever a spin of the roulette wheel; far too many factors lie completely outside your control. And win or lose, red or black, that's it. There's no second place. Still, you persist. Regardless of the odds, and despite the lifestyle, the allure of winning keeps you bound to the process.

Throughout this uncertain existence, however, one thing remains that you can count on. Like an immutable law of physics, there's an unchanging principle of which every actor intent on success should be well aware. Ironically, it's what every professional gambler already knows and lives by: success in wagering depends on consistently reducing risk to a minimum. Once risk is thoroughly minimized, any game of random luck suddenly becomes more of a conscious test of skill. At that point, the odds clearly shift in the professional's favor, placing him or her far ahead of all others playing the same game.

Now you have a chance to transform your auditions into that conscious test of skill. Now you possess the Strategies. Developed out of the shared, real-life experiences of many other actors, the vital information they contain presents a rare opportunity. By studying each Strategy and forging it into an ingrained habit, you can secure the advantages of the master player, placing yourself miles ahead of the competition.

For easy reference, and to help you rapidly obtain the most benefit, the Strategies have been divided into the following three categories: preparation, presentation, and performance.

- *The Preparation Strategies* (nos. 1–31) deal with planning, mental discipline, and attitude—essential requirements for becoming a formidable competitor.

- *The Presentation Strategies* (nos. 32–68) address ways and means of always appearing your best in the casting and interviewing process, such as employing persuasive body language and creating the head shots that sell you best.

- *The Performance Strategies* (nos. 69–101) round out the other categories by providing solid technical advice on craft and, most important, your final delivery in the audition room. These final Strategies reveal secrets that can make all your readings stand out.

You can choose to study the individual Strategies from the very beginning or immediately go to the category where you feel you need the most help. In either case, you'll be well on your way to a brand-new level of achievement: winning more of the parts you genuinely deserve.

THE PREPARATION STRATEGIES

You're running a business, and you're the commodity of that business. If you're going to do that with pride and integrity, you have a lot of work to do.

SHARON STONE

STRATEGY NO.

1

Memorize the "On Any Given Day" Rule

Never forget this all-important rule: "On any given day, any given team, no matter what the odds, can beat another."

It happens all the time. That's why hundreds of thousands of betting dollars are won and lost over professional teams; it's the phenomenon of the upset.

If you're a newer actor, this should increase your determination to press on despite the odds of competing against more experienced actors. If you're experienced, it should serve to warn you never to get lazy.

STRATEGY NO.

2

Fine Instruments Require Constant Care

The best stringed instruments in the world require continual tuning and maintenance. Construction alone cannot elicit the sublime tones produced by careful readjustments. As an extraordinary instrument yourself, you are no different.

If you think you can get by on nothing but appearance or charm, think again. That kind of thing can get you in a door or two and might even get you a job. However, only one thing will get you back into auditions again and again: constant tuning—a conscientious effort to continually refine your skills and reach for new levels of artistic excellence. That's the *real* secret to repeat work in show business.

Study, study, and then study some more.

I jumped over fears, went through emotional glass doors, did everything I could. There wasn't one thing I was afraid to do. And I think you have to come to that point as an actress.

KIM BASINGER

STRATEGY NO.

3

Know What Every Boy Scout Knows

"Be prepared!" Get into the habit of always having a spare picture and résumé (or two). Carry them with you *always*. You never know when you're going to run into someone who might be able to help you.

STRATEGY NO.

4

Unmask the Classic Myth

If you've been buying into the ageless myth of the starving actor, I have just one question: why?

Being an aspiring actor does not necessarily mean being miserable. Nevertheless, countless actors will argue this point, saying that struggling and going hungry is all part of the package, that it's a guaranteed or at least an accepted reality. This kind of sad logic is not only self-defeating but completely unnecessary. (Henry Ford once said that if you argue for your limitations, then sure enough, they're yours!)

In any event, the seemingly elusive solution is simple. Once you identify what actually perpetuates this useless myth in the first place, you're on your way to eating better, paying your bills on time, and all the while pursuing the artistic love of your life.

The trap here is trying to audition for practically everything all the time. Most actors could escape their self-chosen predicament of poverty if they stopped for a moment and examined how acting jobs are ordinarily divided up into two categories, each with its own time frame of operations.

You've probably noticed that plays generally go on at night. Even the rehearsals are normally conducted in the evenings. There can be occasional exceptions, but *most* theatrical work takes place around or outside business hours. Therefore, the solution lies in having a nine-to-five job that will guarantee you a constant paycheck but give you the freedom at night to go after stage work.

Many actors get into financial trouble by jeopardizing their day job. Though their evenings are free to concentrate on theater, they remain unsatisfied with stage work. Finagling time off during business hours to also attend film and TV auditions, they foolishly risk losing their only dependable source of income.

Like stage work, the majority of film and TV jobs fall primarily into a single time frame—in this case, though, the daytime hours. Thus, if you aspire to film and TV roles, you need to have a late-afternoon or evening job. And if possible, ask for weekdays off so you'll be working weekends, leaving two successive days totally free sometime between Monday and Friday.

The key is to decide upon which *single* genre—stage or film—you wish to concentrate on for the time being. Then structure your job hours to coincide with your choice.

Naturally, most actors yearn for film parts. However, your decision must be a logical one based on the time you've already spent in the business. For instance, do you already have enough stage credits to make up a half-decent résumé? If so, don't hesitate to go after the film jobs. But if you're relatively new and don't have too many credits, a lot of doors in the film and TV industry won't be open to you. The best thing in this case is to work a day job for a year or two that will allow you to garner theater credits and build a solid résumé. After that, you just need to change your job hours so you can switch over to film.

That's all there is to it. Having the discipline to make the necessary choices will save you a lot of grief. And, most important, it will keep a lot more change jingling in your pocket.

At the beginning it was all about becoming a student, for me, and pushing myself, and not ever pretending to know something I didn't know about.... It really had to do with my wanting to push the envelope ... to see how far can I go?

TOM CRUISE

STRATEGY NO.

5

Have Confidence

Brand it on your brain, sear it on your chest, or tattoo it on your arm: "Confidence sells." Never forget it. Nearly every result you desire will come from fully understanding this one Phrase.

STRATEGY NO.

6

Find a Second Passion

As an actor, you know how exhilarating it is to learn you've just landed a part. Moreover, you also know the bitter feeling of being turned down approximately nineteen times out of twenty before you're hired. Whether you're a seasoned pro or just a beginner, the fact remains that it's not easy dealing with dashed hopes. Nearly every actor at one time or another falls into this familiar yet vicious trap: no self-esteem.

When you begin to derive your entire sense of fulfillment and personal worth exclusively from the outcome of your auditions, you're in the trap. And you'll always find ample opportunity there to give in to feelings of inadequacy or depression because the number of rejections is *always* larger than the number of jobs you've actually gotten. In essence, you end up postponing the joy of living by waiting for someone else to give you permission to be happy.

Whenever you find the endless rounds of auditions are starting to wear you down, herding you into the trap, take heart. There's an effective remedy. And it starts to work once you take this simple sanity test for actors. It consists only of one, uncomplicated question that you ask yourself: "If the art or craft of acting never even existed, what else would I be doing? What would be my consuming passion?"

Ponder the question carefully and answer it honestly. Your response can have amazing effects. Clearly identifying another worthwhile pursuit impels you to grow in new and different ways by summoning additional, unused resources. In short, it effectively galvanizes your potential into action. Instead of lying around grousing about your down time, when nothing's going on acting-wise, you can set yourself to work on an entirely different but equally stimulating endeavor. Without waiting for permission from anybody, you can jump right into this other life, involving yourself in a fulfilling secondary passion.

What is your secondary passion? Dancing? Music? Writing? How about even starting your own business? One actor used his down time to rescue lost pets from the ravines and canyons surrounding Los Angeles. He turned out to be quite successful at it and later founded a society that drew the attention and financial support of many celebrities.

Why not protect yourself from the self-esteem trap right this moment? Elect to take the test before proceeding into the other Strategies. Once you've identified your other passion, you'll begin to have insights into fresh plans or activities you can get involved in at a moment's notice. You'll be surprised how quickly any distress you feel over an audition that's failed to come through will evaporate in the face of your other pursuit. And, most important, you'll keep your sanity. Never again will you have to wait for the powers that be to say when you're allowed to feel good about yourself.

What's carried me through from the very beginning is a clarity of direction. When I set my sights on what I want, I go full force, with patience, perseverance, and passion.

DEMI MOORE

STRATEGY NO.

Recognize the Passkey to Professionalism

One of the worst things you can do after auditioning is kick yourself for not having done a better job. Okay, you're only human—you feel you have to chastise yourself a bit. But it's not going to do you one bit of good to dwell on failure to the extent of letting it ruin your whole day—or week.

So you screwed up. It's no different than a professional baseball player who strikes out at the plate. He doesn't enjoy striking out any more than you do. What makes him a professional, however, is that he'll use it as a way to analyze and strengthen his game. So figure out where exactly you went wrong and resolve to improve your game. Maintaining an audition diary might even prove helpful. Remember: amateurs never stop dreaming; professionals never stop learning.

STRATEGY NO.

8

Do Push-Ups and Sit-Ups for the Eyes

Ever exercise your cold-reading motor skills? Far too many actors neglect or overlook them entirely. Yet they make up the single most important feature of acting. After all, you can't look forward to being on any film set unless you first look good in the office. That requires staying off the page as much as possible, fully engaging the other reader during your audition.

The preparation it takes to be an able cold reader is not unlike the discipline necessary for developing muscles. You not only need to develop them in order to win more auditions, you need to practice regularly to keep them consistently strong.

Here's how: If you don't have a script available, find a book and make sure the type size on its pages is somewhat close to that on scripts, but *never* larger. Then designate a single point on your wall as a visual target. (A light switch makes a good one if you're seated.) Begin by looking down and silently reading at least three or four words from a line or sentence. Then look up and deliver those words out loud only at your target.

It doesn't matter if you can only pick up a few words at first. In a very short while, you'll begin to notice you can pick up more words with little difficulty. And within three or four weeks, you'll clearly see a vast difference. Not only will you be able to pick up entire sentences, but the speed at which you do so will increase.

In most cases, ten to fifteen minutes a day is sufficient. Less than ten minutes hardly helps, while more than fifteen invariably strains the eyes. If you'd like to accelerate your progress, do this exercise once in the morning and once in the evening.

Cold reading may not be acting per se, but don't forget that acting is exactly like professional sports: your game is only as good as your fundamentals.

Plan your work, work your plan. Lack of system produces that 'I'm swamped' feeling.

EDWARD NORTON

STRATEGY NO.

9

Put a Real Job before Your Reel Job

Always have some reliable outside job or source of income that allows you to pursue your craft without having to sell one of your kidneys. Going into an audition desperately needing the gig has serious consequences. Not only can you count on your anxiety actually dulling your talent, but you can be sure your auditioners will be able to smell it. Whether you call it an odor or a vibe, the people casting you will pick up on your desperation. And that starts them on the road to the three-step process best described as Rejection Logic:

Thought no. 1: "Hmmm, this actor is unduly anxious."

Thought no. 2: "It probably means he can't get work."

Thought no. 3: "Can't get work? Oh God, a bad actor! Red alert! Reject! Reject!"

STRATEGY NO.

10

Develop Your Voice

It has been said, and rightly, that your voice is your second face. A pleasant, resonant voice is attractive. Having a refined pitch and prominent resonance is unquestionably a good way to enhance your presence and greatly improve your chances in the audition room. Not only is a trained voice a mark of experience, but TV and film directors know that a resonant voice is a technical asset: it records better.

Studying and developing your voice therefore, is a must, not a maybe. If this book contained only two Strategies, they would be about practicing your craft and developing your voice.

Through my own experiences and achievements, I have found that no amount of encouragement, help, or advice can make an unmotivated person a star, while at the same time, no amount of failure, discouragement, or adversity can dissuade a determined actor.

SUSAN SAINT JAMES

STRATEGY NO.

11

Harness the Power of Habit

Have you ever heard or used the expression, "I couldn't help it—force of habit"? Never underestimate the potential of that force. We hardly think of it as a potential for anything because the phrase usually arises from doing things with negative associations, such as thoughtless behavior or careless blunders. Yet the results that can arise from harnessing *productive* habitual behavior can be downright astonishing.

Most people succeed in achieving extraordinary things not so much because of grand schemes and dreams, but by the cumulative power of constructive daily habits. Consistent, positive actions taken day by day, no matter how small or how few, often count for more than the most thorough plans.

Say you wanted to be a novelist. If you got into the simple habit of writing just one page a day, you'd have 365 pages at the end of the year—a novel-sized piece of work, for sure!

As an actor, you might want to start out with a pad and pencil along with your morning cup of coffee (or whatever you usually have). During the time it takes to finish the coffee, you could list twelve different things you could do to either promote yourself or gain work. If you did that simple task daily, without fail, in a year's time you'd wind up with over four thousand ideas on how to get ahead.

STRATEGY NO.

12

Analyze Your Batting Average

Are you ever satisfied with the ratio of work gained to work auditioned for? It's no secret that most actors aren't. However, a little examination of your own statistics might help improve them.

For instance, if you've been going out for a large number of readings but haven't booked anything in a long time, there's very likely a weak area you're not fully aware of. You can remedy the situation right away by asking your agent to get some feedback from the casting directors you've been reading for lately. Armed with that information, notify your acting coach and let him or her work closely with you on your particular problem. If you don't currently have an acting instructor, seek out someone with an established reputation and discuss it with him or her. At the very least, a competent instructor can assess your performance with a far more detached and objective eye.

What you have to have inside you in this business, because it is so ruthless, is a burning desire to be an actor. In this business, you have to be driven.

BEN KINGSLEY

STRATEGY NO.

13

Hold On to Your Chance Card

If you're a relatively new actor and often find yourself in the waiting room along with recognizable "heavyweights" (actors with a lot of credits), don't throw in the towel just yet. Remember that in this very unpredictable business, the possibility of your being hired over one of these more experienced actors is not at all out of the question. Why else would you have been called in?

The truth of the matter is, your photo caught the interest of the casting director. And by actually making the effort to schedule you for an audition, he or she is saying, "We're willing to take a chance on you, newcomer." TV and film have voracious appetites for new faces. (Take another look at the first Strategy.)

STRATEGY NO.

14

Don't Forget That All-Essential Notebook

As in any other business, staying organized is critical to your success. Therefore, no actor should be without his or her notebook, calendar, or day planner.

Something fairly large, such as a folding writing pad with pockets or a binder that closes with a zipper, is best. It will hold your things together as you fly from one audition to another. It's useful to have one with a pocket or two large enough for you to keep your sides (a few pages from the script), commercial ad copy, and head shots all in one convenient place.

Besides a calendar, your notebook should also contain paper for jotting down notes, addresses, and the like. A map of the city is also a great resource to carry along. And of course, make sure your notebook always contains a few more pictures and résumés than you think you'll actually need.

If you see yourself being an actor till the day you die, and living a healthy life, then that is the moment you truly take responsibility for your technique.

FRANCES MCDORMAND

STRATEGY NO.

15

Determine Your Determination

The most predictable thing about show business is that it's unpredictable. It possesses a crazy side that can lead you to dining on four-star French cuisine one month and force you into peanut butter and jelly for the next five. How much you make and how often you work are based on so many random conditions, you'd swear a lunatic actually made up the rules.

This is the predominant drawback of your profession: irregular work at irregular pay. And every bit of the attraction and glamour can fade during the long, unanticipated stretches of joblessness.

The key to successfully enduring the hazardous ups and downs lies in your attitude toward your goals. It's not enough to have them. And it's not enough to take action on them. But it's essential to believe in them.

A Hollywood talent manager once said he was absolutely convinced, after many years in the film and TV industry, of one thing: actors who are fiercely determined to get ahead *will* get ahead. Nothing, he said, will ever serve performers more than sheer persistence. A steadfast attitude that doesn't recognize setbacks practically voids all other attributes—including looks and talent.

STRATEGY NO.

16

Temper Enthusiasm with Business Sense

New actors often overlook the necessity of doing things in a logical, properly conceived order. As a result, they often engage in a classic form of self-sabotage activity that could be called "getting to market before the crop's ready." In their excitement and enthusiasm to get ahead, they manage actually to severely impede rather than accelerate their progress.

To begin with, what do you suppose most agents consider the highest priority with respect to securing work for their clients? It's not difficult to figure out when you consider that an actor would have to work nearly a whole month on an Equity stage before he or she could make the same kind of money gotten from working a mere day or two on a TV series or film. In plain language, the good bucks are made around cameras. Thus, one of the best things actors can do for themselves is make sure they have a rock-solid foundation in film acting technique.

Unfortunately, a lot of beginning actors don't see things this way. They think acting is acting—that it's all the same. Having done a fair number of plays and dabbled in a workshop or two, they charge headlong into the film and TV job market. If they do this before they thoroughly grasp the distinct refinements of film acting, they fall flat on their face in auditions by giving inconsistent readings—scenes punctuated by glaring moments of over-the-top reactions. If word subsequently gets back to their agents (as it usually does) that they need more training, then what possible incentive would those agents have for getting them more auditions?

These impatient actors fail to see the big picture. It could be well over a year before casting directors would take another chance on seeing someone who essentially wasted their time.

Moral of this story? The industry is too tightly knit, and casting directors' memories too long, for you to make the costly error of getting out into the market too soon. Casting directors compare notes, especially about newcomers. If your name comes up during their conversations, you'll want it to be for the right reasons.

Set goals. Get a job. Enroll in acting classes. Get a head shot. Pound the pavement. Get an agent. Make it happen.
ALEC BALDWIN

STRATEGY NO.

17

Save Your Breath on Accents

Many beginning actors express serious concerns over whether or not they should be studying accents. The days of actors doing other nationalities are practically over. There are so many performers in the competitive arena now, you can forget about doing a French waiter or a British diplomat, because the casting director will likely find a real French or English actor for the job. If you've been raised in the Midwest and are called upon to do a Bostonian accent, you'll more than likely be aced out by someone from the North Atlantic region. In fact, it's gotten so crazy that if a producer puts out a call that he's looking for a Ukrainian dwarf who juggles chainsaws, one will arrive the following day, with a bag of chain saws, ready to go.

The probability of needing to stay current in an accent or two doesn't truly warrant the effort. Working on improving the pitch and resonance of your normal voice is a much better investment of your time.

There is an exception, however. If you actually appear undeniably ethnic and don't have the accent that would fit the look, it would certainly be prudent to work on one.

STRATEGY NO.

18

Shun the Slow Boat to China

Nearly every performers' union compiles various statistics on the industry. The most sobering ones are the unemployment figures from the Screen Actors Guild. At any given time, nearly 95 percent of the membership is unemployed. To compound that distressing situation, many new actors enter the profession every year, competing for an ever-shrinking number of jobs.

If the only effort you make to get work is soaking up rays by the poolside and waiting for your agent to call, then you're making a bad mistake. "Waiting to be discovered" is the slowest boat there is. If you want to be a busier actor, then you'd better get busy right now.

There are other ways besides the audition process to get your name and face out there. Just ask around. There are actors' networks and rap groups. There are showcases that allow you to meet and perform scenes for industry people. There are professional trade symposiums that you can attend and where you can drop off pictures. And you can ask your agent to set you up with a pre-screen or general interview with the casting people you haven't yet been able to see.

Be inventive. There's no limit to the number of ways you can stay visible. Just pick up a good book on show-business public relations and you'll see. The bottom line is, you've got to hustle. Your face and name have to be in many places as many times as possible.

When you've learned how to draw on your subconscious powers, there's really no limit to what you can accomplish. You often find, to your surprise, that you're acting better than you know how.

ANGELA LANSBURY

STRATEGY NO.
19

Don't Go It Alone

If you think you can get far without an agent, think again. Not only does an agent have the clout to open doors for you that would otherwise be closed, but he or she stands between you and industry executives, protecting your interests.

Also, casting directors negotiate with agents because they don't like to negotiate with actors directly. It's just too unpleasant a process and often not an altogether objective one, either.

Whoever came up with the phrase "self-representation" probably gave up in the quest for a competent agent. Don't make that mistake. In blunt terms, self-representation is a pastime for the delusional.

STRATEGY NO.
20

Get a Lot of Bang for Your Buck

If you'd like to make your training dollars go further, look into courses conducted by casting directors, especially if you haven't been able to see them otherwise. By studying with competent casting people, you'll not only get some inside-track informa-tion, but you'll also become acquainted with what that particular person specifically looks for in auditions. And if you do quite well in the class, there's a very good chance that same casting director could soon call you in for a reading.

But there's a huge drawback lurking in the shadows. Attending this kind of workshop before you've had some decent training and experience will actually do you more harm than good. If you display weakness or inconsistency in your scene work with these casting directors, they'll only remember one thing about you: not to have you read for one of their client producers or directors. A casting director's ongoing success is based on finding strong, interesting actors for his or her clients. The last thing he or she needs is to be embarrassed by an overly eager actor's wavering attempts in front of these clients.

That's the caveat: don't attend one of these workshops unless you're extremely confident in your abilities. If you are, well and good. Get in and get seen. It will be money well spent. If you're not entirely sure, get more training.

I could've let go years ago and whatever abilities I had would have been there. Everything. I didn't have to hang on so tightly. That was the beginning of the change. And the event was joyous.

ALAN ARKIN

STRATEGY NO.

21

Fail to Plan and You Plan to Fail

Despite the hype, glamour, and other trappings of show busi-ness, it's still a business. And it's one of the most competitive in the world. Getting anywhere in it takes indefatigable effort and, above all, planning. If you lack a concerted plan and just run from one workshop, showcase, or play to another, you end up feeling busy but not getting any business done.

Learn to set realistic goals and, most especially, priorities. There's so much work involved in advancing yourself as an actor that if you don't adopt these essential skills right away, you might as well go back home or learn to be content with community theater the rest of your life.

What are your short-term goals? Your long-term goals? Do you have weekly or monthly objectives? If this idea is new to you, it's time you did a little studying.

There are a number of impressive books on the subject written by consultants and time-management experts. A couple of classics are *Think and Grow Rich,* by Napoleon Hill, and *How to Get Control of Your Time and Life,* by Alan Lakein. No self-respecting actor should be without at least these two.

STRATEGY NO.

22

Think Twice about Cattle Calls

You haven't completely paid your dues until you've experienced one of these crazy events. In place of a firm appointment time for a set number of actors, a cattle call (aptly named by those who've experienced them) is an openly advertised casting session for any and all actors who want to attend. Instead of a nice, sane number like, say, twenty or thirty people competing for a role, a cattle call can produce upward of five or six hundred actors!

If you're willing to stand in a line that wraps around the studio twice and ends in Wisconsin, more power to you. However, before you spend half your life doing so, you should mull a few things over.

You have to weigh the time spent against the possible outcome. After all, the chances of succeeding against such ludicrous numbers are slim indeed. The biggest downside to all of this is the possibility that a production company is holding a large, open call for one reason alone: promotion. By announcing that they're "looking for that new, special person," the company can get into the papers or on the evening news, garnering free advance publicity for the film. It may not sound fair, but it happens. And it will doubtless continue to happen as long as there are enough Hollywood hopefuls willing to play along.

If, however, the open casting call is indeed legitimate, you may have a slight chance if you know that what they're looking for is pretty much what you look like. Another remote hope is if they're looking for several types rather than just one character. Otherwise, consider this form of open call nothing more than a day wasted.

Before you actually take a deep breath and take the plunge, ask yourself if there's some other career-benefiting activity someplace else, somewhere you could be making more effective use of your time. For example, you might have a better chance of securing future work or readings by attending an industry seminar conducted by a casting panel. Quite often, people on these panels will field questions and later on look over pictures and résumés. (They're often advertised in the trade papers or in union offices.)

Maybe you could call your agent and schedule some time to discuss mutual concerns. There are a number of things you can do that will ultimately serve you better. Just give it some careful thought before you join the studio stampede.

Like any artist, the actor has to be open to inspiration, intuition, and the unconscious. When you know what you're looking for, that's all you get—what's previously known. But when you're open to what's possible, you get something new, and that's creativity.

ALAN ALDA

STRATEGY NO.

23

Don't Take It Personally

Having chosen the life of an actor, you must face rejection over and over again. People try to be helpful, telling you, "Don't take it personally—they're selecting, not rejecting." Even so, it still feels like rejection. And that feels like hell. Yet, if you're firmly determined to persevere, you'll eventually master absorbing the inevitable lumps and bumps. And the sooner you do, the better off you'll be.

One dependable way is by viewing your setbacks in an aggressive, analytical way—not a passive, regretful one. A good example comes from professional sports, which is not at all unlike acting. It takes many, many hours of practice for just a few hours of professional play. And winning is never guaranteed.

When you've lost a part because of a not-so-hot reading, think like a pro who's lost a game. Make mental notes, resolving to overcome mistakes. Like any professional ball player, you want to concentrate solely on improvement—where you have to go, not where you've been. Dwelling entirely on failure only precipitates more of it.

STRATEGY NO.

24

Learn to Hunt

The irony of your profession is that you'll spend more time attempting to work than actually working. In fact, if you made a pie chart of all the time you spend in activities having to do with developing your career, it would look something like this: Picture in your mind the thinnest slice you could possibly cut out of it. That represents the actual time you spend genuinely working at a paying acting job. (This, of course, presupposes you're like 90 percent of all actors.) As for the remainder of the pie, you can divide it approximately in half. One of those halves is representative of the time you spend, or should spend, in training and refining your skills. The other half is the most critical portion of the pie. It's the time you need to be looking for, auditioning for, or attempting to create more work.

That's the message of the chart. Improving your ability to obtain work is just as vital as improving your ability to act. You have to be as much a hunter as you are a performer.

Naturally, your agent is supposed to do a lot of that for you, but he or she cannot possibly keep track of every possible independent venture that's going on. Your agent's usual casting information is typically limited to the breakdown services, which tend to post the higher-budget projects. So unless you relish your thin slice of the pie, you have to aggressively track all possible prospects of getting more work.

A good place to start hunting is your union office. Often casting notices for small, independent projects are posted there that aren't normally in your agent's breakdowns. In addition, the unions frequently sponsor seminars that feature key industry people, such as casting directors and producers. Attending one of the smaller gatherings can be real plus. In a tiny, friendlier circle, you can spend time getting to know the kind of people essential to helping you get ahead. And if you're lucky, they just might be involved at that time in something you'd be right for.

Another proven way to stay abreast of work opportunities is to habitually read what are known in the business as "the trades." These are insider-type newspapers or magazines devoted exclusively to the business side of entertainment. From time to time they also list casting and seminar notices.

Presently, there's a terrific one in North America devoted to providing more work for actors. It's called *Backstage West,* and each week it lists a substantial number of new casting notices. The auditions are predominantly in Los Angeles, but there are occasional notices for New York and other major metropolitan areas.

Two other periodicals can be helpful to the alert hunter. *Daily Variety* and *Hollywood Reporter* are the most widely read publications in the business. The main function of these two popular trades lies in providing current, newsworthy items that impact the entire industry, not just acting. Consequently, they list only a limited number of casting notices. However, they furnish a lot of the most recent development and production information. And that's a good starting point to ferret out potential work leads. For example, whenever projects are listed as being in development (films and TV shows that are in the preparation stages), the trades also list the personnel involved. Since these projects are in the preparatory phase, there's a good chance that not all parts are cast yet.

Look over the list of people associated with the project to see if it includes some producer, crew member, or actor you've worked with in the past. If you're lucky, some friend of yours might be involved. If either is the case, don't hesitate to send in a picture and résumé and attach a very brief cover letter. Keep it friendly and get to the point. For instance, after you've completed the "Hi, how have you been?" part, mention that you saw the production announcement and were wondering whether there might be something you could come in and read for.

This Strategy has provided you with five potential sources besides your agent to help you capture more acting opportunities. Be a smart hunter. Learn to track down even more.

I would say that acting is one of the toughest jobs in the world to get. You have to be really focused on it, and you've got to do it for the right reasons. Not to be famous or rich, but because that's what interests and moves you.

HARRISON FORD

STRATEGY NO.

25

Get Acquainted with the Naked Truth

There's no disputing the fact that pornographic films make a lot of money. Another reality about this particular part of the industry is the virtual permanence of just such a career choice. If you decide to start auditioning for them, prepare to remain in them. Because as of this writing, there are still no pornographic stars who've made a complete and successful transition to legitimate work.

While industry people may (and I strongly emphasize "may") forgive you for making one of these films as an alternative to starving to death, they will never absolve you of two or more. At that point, you've irreversibly become a porno pro.

STRATEGY NO.

26

Don't Give Away Your Power

Constantly and arbitrarily talking about what you do is a subtle trap. Naturally, you love your craft, but ceaselessly discussing your auditions and your acting work with a number of people does very little except feed the insatiable beast called Lack of Confidence. (If you ask an insecure actor how he or she is, be prepared to listen to a résumé.)

It's wise to talk with knowledgeable professionals about overcoming difficulties or improving your skills. But engaging in endless conversations with your grocer, your neighbor, and anyone else willing to listen undermines any deep personal sense that you're good enough to do what you want to do. Don't give away your power by giving in to your ego. Strive rather to reinforce your vision in order to make it a reality. That takes worthwhile actions, not idle words.

I had to learn to trust myself.

MELANIE GRIFFITH

STRATEGY NO.

27

Capitalize on the Commercial Advantage

More than any other professional venue for acting, commercials offer inexperienced actors the best opportunity for breaking into the business. Producers and directors are more apt to take a chance on a rookie simply because they're always on the lookout for brand-new faces. And not only do TV commercials pay well, but they're also an unbeatable showcase. Several actors have gotten their careers off the ground through the constant exposure of a good commercial.

Developing strong commercial-audition skills is consequently a wise investment of your time and energy. If you can find an excellent workshop, get in as soon as you can—you'll multiply your newcomer's advantage even more. Take a minimum of two courses—one from a working commercial casting director and one from a working commercial actor. You'll get a realistic and sensible perspective that comes from both sides of the camera, which will equip you with a keener competitive edge. In the meantime, the next Strategy will furnish information to help sharpen that edge right now.

STRATEGY NO.

28

Apply the Rule of Threes

Figuring out exactly what to do in order to give a strong commercial audition can be challenging. It's not just a simple matter of smiling while saying the product name and hoping for the best. There are critical elements of style, for instance, that must color your delivery, dependent upon the type of commercial you're trying out for. If you're familiar with the commercial type and demonstrate its distinctive style, you'll obviously do well. But if those elements are missing, you needn't bother writing down the shooting date in your calendar.

Here's a useful shorthand tool for clarifying your needs and keeping you a step ahead of the competition. It breaks commercials down in three stages, enabling you to classify the commercial, develop the requisite performance, and ultimately refine the delivery. Each commercial classification has three specific criteria of style—hence the "Rule of Threes." Let's look at this tool in detail and cite some examples:

STEP 1: CLASSIFY THE TYPE OF COMMERCIAL

Commercials can be broken down into just three basic types. There's the *product-spokesperson* spot, the *slice-of-life* spot, and the *classic* spot. ("Spot" is industry jargon for commercial.) Any other commercial is nothing more than a variation or combination of these three.

In the prestigious product-spokesperson spot, you're the only one (besides the product) in the commercial. It's your job and yours alone to sell the product.

In the slice-of-life spot, you perform ordinary routines such as shopping at a store, eating at a restaurant, working at your job, or engaging in recreation with family or friends. In most cases, this kind of spot has a separate narrator, meaning of course, you'll have no dialogue.

The classic spot truly deserves its name, having been around since TV began. In this type of commercial, a problem is presented, such as, for example, a large stain in your beautiful carpet. Then the product is introduced, after which comes the resolution: the product makes short work of the nasty stain, and presto—life is now worth living.

STEP 2: DEVELOP YOUR DELIVERY ACCORDING TO TYPE
If you're auditioning for a product-spokesperson spot, you'll want to effect a delivery that exudes a polished sense of authority.

If you're going out for the slice-of-life spot, all you need concentrate on is going through familiar, real-life activities in an unaffected, good-natured way. (How could you shop with authority?)

Your delivery in the classic spot is a little more complex because it involves carefully orchestrating your moods. For example, you'll need to display frustration during the beginning, problem portion. Then you should indicate grateful amazement during the clean-up or resolution stage. Finally, you should end the spot with an expression that clearly demonstrates that a bottle of Stain-Be-Gone is the best friend you ever had.

STEP 3: REFINE YOUR PERFORMANCE ACCORDING TO ENVIRONMENT
In the product-spokesperson spot, you need to fine-tune your authority by adding some personal warmth. However, your surroundings will dictate just how much. In a clinical setting, for instance, you might be wearing a white lab coat and pitching aspirin. You would want, on balance, lots of authority and a little warmth.

In a corporate environment, where you'd wear a suit and sell something such as financial services or long-distance phone service, you'd do better with more warmth than authority.

A third, less common style for the product spokesperson is the comedic one. Producers often look for a comedian to fill such a role. But if, during your audition, your timing is good and you genuinely entertain the room, your chances are just as good as any comic's.

In the slice-of-life spot, you simply affect a moderate amount of cheerfulness as you go about your business or work. If you don't, you'll appear too somber—especially on videotape. If you're shopping or eating, you'll want to represent an even higher level of joy. And finally, if you're playing games or sports with others, you'd do well to cut loose with over-the-top gusto.

Classic spot adjustments rely heavily on shot distance. That is, the projection and transition of your emotions depend on how close you are to the camera. Once again, you are faced with three choices. If there's an intimate close-up of your face, you don't want to do anything but "think" your transitions, not project them. Simple, economic acting is the key. No mugging! On the other hand, if the product or logo is in the foreground while you're in the background, then making larger moves is definitely in order. Even some comic mugging is not totally out of place in a longer shot such as this. Lastly, if both you and the product are close together, in the same shot, then moderate projection is called for.

To conclude this Strategy on analyzing your commercial preparation, it's important to briefly mention the storyboard. The storyboard is the best possible indication of what the entire commercial should look like, short of actually filming it. It's normally posted in the waiting room and consists of a poster or bulletin board with a series of 8½-by-11-inch sheets of paper attached to it. On the sheets are hand-rendered sketches from the ad agency that designed the spot you're about to audition for. The sketches detail the sequence of events and activities in the commercial. If there's dialogue, that too will be included, posted to the left of the illustrations.

Remember always to look for and consult the storyboard at every commercial audition. Next to your commercial sides, it's the best thing for confirming the choices you've derived from applying the Rule of Threes.

Be ready so you can grasp opportunity when it comes.
CHARLES BRONSON

STRATEGY NO.

29

Make Field Notes

Don't just chalk up a lost role to the usual excuses (too young, too old, too short, etc.) Distressing as your losses may seem, they're still a prominent part of your professional growth.

In the first few years of auditioning, it's worth your time to maintain some kind of brief audition diary—basically a tally sheet of wins and losses, with pertinent footnotes. Keeping this kind of self-assessing scorecard makes it possible for you to focus on what's working and what needs attention.

STRATEGY NO.

30

Hire an Electric Secretary

Got an answering machine or answering service? Next to his or her pictures, it's an actor's most vital tool. If you don't have one, you're going to cut down your career before it's even had a chance to sprout.

For instance, if you're at work or you've just stepped out to the store, how is anyone going to reach you with critical information such as "You're in the callbacks—they want to see you today at 2 P.M." or "Your call time and location have been changed"?

Pagers or cellular phones are also wise investments. But save your money and get the answering service first. The other devices are for later, when your rate of calls clearly begins to increase.

I never got a job I didn't create for myself.

RUTH GORDON

STRATEGY NO.

31

Rules Were Meant to Be Broken

Keep in mind that much of the information these Strategies contain refers to options—the Strategies aren't holy commandments forever etched in stone. There can be exceptions. Only time and experience will tell you when to bend or break some of these rules.

If you break a rule before truly knowing what you're doing, your chances of landing the part fall somewhere within the proverbial slim-to-none region. Until then, get out to as many auditions as possible and endeavor to take away something instructive from each and every one of them—win or lose.

THE PRESENTATION STRATEGIES

What I try to remember is that my life is a gift, and so I don't want to miss it by accommodating everybody else's wishes. I want to try to find out what I believe is good and true for myself and try to give that rather than accommodate myself into oblivion.

WILLIAM HURT

STRATEGY NO.

32

Check Your Posture at the Door

What kind of unspoken signals do you broadcast when you walk into the audition room? Your bearing—the way you hold your head and shoulders—can make a world of difference.

For example, if you make your entrance with your head slightly down and your back or shoulders a little stooped, it advertises that you're used to being defeated. If, on the other hand, your head is high and your shoulders are back, your posture reflects an abundance of confidence. It announces, "Here's someone poised for another victory."

Take some time out to check your posture and the way you walk. You might even get a friend to watch you and provide some objective feedback. Remember: the more you walk in like a winner, the more you'll walk out winning.

STRATEGY NO.

33

Smile When You Say That

Make it a habit to treat everyone you meet in the studios and offices with sincere respect and courtesy. It's not only the hallmark of a genuine professional, but it's also a kind of performer's insurance policy. The fast-track game of promotions and shake-ups in the film industry means that today's secretary can be tomorrow's casting director. Need I say any more?

Nothing is impossible. "Impossible" just takes a few more phone calls.

MICHAEL J. FOX

STRATEGY NO.

34

Know Your Niche

The giant casting machine is a conservative piece of equipment. The cautious selections it makes are based not on talent alone, but on prevailing or popular notions as well.

Your appearance, from the way you dress and speak to the way you carry yourself, is what's called your "type" or niche. It's what the people who run the machine use to instantly classify you and your acting style. More often than not, your niche coincides with someone currently in the mainstream. Casting directors and producers use popular presumptions to identify you. For instance, if you're a woman, you might be either an impulsive, passionate Anne Heche type or—the opposite—a reflective

Meryl Streep type. A man might be viewed as a low-key, somewhat self-effacing type like Tobey Maguire or a rebellious, edgy Matt Dillon type. What this boils down to is the fact that a Matt Dillon wouldn't normally be cast as a country boy because his mannerisms wouldn't be plausible. Likewise, it would be difficult to accept Tobey Maguire as an inner-city gang leader.

You might say this is safe, uncreative image casting, not acting casting. And you might be right. But that's the way it works. Knowing your niche, therefore, is essential to landing more parts.

Up to now, you may have thought of yourself as a leading man, but your quirkiness may put you in the niche of a comic relief player. If you're a female, you might think you've been perceived as a professional career woman, but your soft, wholesome features make you look more like a young mother. Playing to ways that oppose how you're viewed hampers your chances. The conservative machine can't get a fix on just who you are and, consequently, what role you're truly appropriate for.

If you're not absolutely sure about your niche, ask other actors and especially your agent how you come across. If you can obtain a clear picture of this, you can enhance your performances by gracefully playing along with that picture, not undermining your efforts by struggling against it. And, just as important, you can arrange for your head shots to play into this whole niche aspect by dressing in an appropriate style for your photo shoot.

STRATEGY NO.

35

Know Who Your Real Fans Are

Want to feel a little more confident in your auditions? Then get acquainted with this bit of good news: casting directors are actually your first genuine fans. They're rooting for you to be the best you can possibly be. That's no exaggeration. For one thing, their credibility as finders of talent depends upon how well the talent does. If too many actors do poorly, that casting director will soon be out of a job. And for another, being at your absolute best makes their job easier. The sooner they find someone who's right for the part, the sooner they can get on to other responsibilities.

I was always scrambling to please people. Then a funny thing occurred to me: To be a human being who's at peace in her skin is comforting to everyone who sees you. And to be at peace, you have to be yourself.

MERCEDES RUEHL

STRATEGY NO.

36

Get In, Get Out, and Don't Dawdle

Sometimes after a reading the casting people will ask about your availability or your sizes. If so, let them know. If not, smile, say thank you, and *leave the room*. Don't loiter in an effort to volunteer more information. Even worse, don't make ingratiating remarks such as "I really appreciated being able to read for you." Excessive niceness backfires on you by exposing an underlying emotional neediness. You might as well ask them if you can polish their shoes. (Review Strategy no. 5.)

STRATEGY NO.

37

Don't Overlook Your Grooming

Do you have a lint brush? If not, why not? Nothing looks worse than walking into a room in a nice wool sports coat or skirt that looks like something you share with the cat. Scuffed shoes or dirty fingernails won't win you any points either, unless, of course, they're indisputably part of your character.

Always make sure your clothes are clean and pressed. Bottom line: if you look like you desperately need the job, chances are pretty good you won't get it.

Success is going from failure to failure without losing enthusiasm.

DANNY GLOVER

STRATEGY NO.

38

Get Rid of the Magazine

Nothing smacks more of inexperience in a reading than an actor who keeps his or her head down, eyes glued to the script as if it were an engrossing magazine article.

To look as professional as possible, always keep your face up and your attention fixed on the person you're reading with. When you need to get your line, use *only your eyes* to pick it up. If you don't use just your eyes, your head will continually bob up and down in a very distracting way. That's nearly as detrimental as the magazine style.

STRATEGY NO.

39

Look Out for Numero Uno

Always remember to do a last-minute check of your appearance prior to actually reading. Duck into a bathroom and make sure your hair didn't do something funny in your mad rush to get there. Also, look for any surprises your teeth or nostrils may be holding in store for you.

You make the wrong choices and there are ramifications. But through all of that, and the pain and the experiences, there comes a deeper understanding of yourself.
NICOLE KIDMAN

STRATEGY NO.

40

Stay Upbeat to Stay in the Running

Being positive during the interview part of your audition is imperative. Nobody wants to hear how you struggled through traffic to get there, how hard it was to find the place, how your car broke down, and on and on. People involved in casting lead hectic lives, and like you and everyone else, they have problems, too. You don't score points by talking about your own.

When you get to your audition, make sure you've shaken off any negative influences that might have been upsetting you that day. Forget the car trouble and other pressures for now. In order to be at your absolute best, you've got to be in a vibrant, upbeat frame of mind.

A remarkable exercise to help you get there is to take a lively inventory of yourself. Before your interview, find five accomplishments from your past, recent or distant, that you're genuinely proud of. Count off on your fingers, one by one, things that spring to mind as uplifting, stand-out events in your life.

For instance, think about the last time you landed a part. Or maybe something you did completely outside of the industry that made you feel great for having done it. Did you get involved with any volunteer work? Help somebody in need? Get a home run at a company picnic baseball game? Most important, you must not only see these things, you must also revive the original feelings that went with them.

This exercise may seem overly simplistic, but the goal is to reset your thinking and stimulate your entire physiology as well. Reliving life-affirming moments sends signals into the body, generating exceptional effects. It revitalizes your speech with a tendency to use more resourceful language and actually straightens your posture as well. If there's such a thing as magic, this exercise performs it.

The entire process shouldn't take long. Fifteen seconds to half a minute to relive each circumstance is usually sufficient. With a little practice, you may even find the experience so enjoyable you'll get into the habit of doing it any time you face a personal challenge.

STRATEGY NO.

41

Look Better to Do Better

When it comes to wardrobe, you'll find most auditions require a generic look—that is, normal everyday attire. For example, you may hear from your agent, "They're looking for an upscale casual look." So if you spend any money on yourself, make sure that clothing tops your list, right after rent and food.

You naturally want to present your best side, and always having crisp, new-looking clothes is your guarantee. If you're really strapped for cash, however, then do a lot of your errands and running around only in your well-used clothes. Allow them to take the further wear and tear so you can set aside a few pristine articles strictly for auditions. You'll do better if you feel better. Looking like you don't need the money generates confidence not only in yourself, but in those considering you for a part.

Sometimes you do your best work in the worst circumstances. You learn to get a certain focus and certain belief in yourself. You realize your goals clearly: what you're doing, why you're trying to get there.

FORREST WHITAKER

STRATEGY NO.

42

Adopt the *En garde!* Stance

Instantly snapping your script into the most advantageous reading position, with a minimum of movement and hesitation just before you begin your audition, radiates self-assurance. It's almost as if you're confidently declaring, *"En garde!"* And once your script is in position, make every attempt to keep it there. Bringing it up to your face each time for a line, then lowering it, then bringing it up and lowering it again is a monotonous habit that invariably distracts those watching you. Your poise will seem far more professional if you keep your script in one spot.

What's the best spot? Directly in front of you. That minimizes sideways head movement, allowing you to pick up your lines with just your eyes. Also, the top edge of your script should never be higher than the imaginary plane established by your chin. Picture the end of a ruler taped under your chin and extending forward, away from your face. You don't want the top of your script to be above the ruler. With every little bit that it rises, it hides that much more of your face. And if it does, the casting committee and/or camera will be deprived of a complete view of all your features and expressions as you read.

Because of the unavoidable tension of an audition, you may not always have your script in the most advantageous position. But if you've practiced riveting your script in one spot based on these key angles, you'll never have to give it a second thought. It will have become a habit, and you'll do it automatically despite the pressure of any last-minute notes or changes given to you just before you read. You can launch right into your reading— *en garde!*—with your face completely open. And regardless of whether a casting committee sits on the right, on the left, or in the middle of the room, you'll always guarantee them a good view.

STRATEGY NO.

43

Correspond Sparingly

Should you send a thank-you note to casting directors after auditions in order to be remembered? It's up you, but the truth of the matter is this: if your work wasn't memorable, what makes you think a thank-you card will help matters? In most cases, it will only serve to remind them of your weak reading. If, however, your audition was strong, it's highly doubtful you'll be forgotten.

The best time to send a thank-you note is when you get the job. It's not just courteous, but impressively professional. Being remembered for that is practically guaranteed.

I believe in the toughness of actors. I have a genuine pride in actors as my people. We're often called egomaniacs, irresponsible, stupid, unaware, and kind of a joke. We're accused of having big egos. Well, the actor's ego is no different in size because he's an actor. A writer or a painter or a musician can go off into a corner and lick his wounds, but an actor stands out in front of a crowd and takes it.

MAUREEN STAPLETON

STRATEGY NO.

44

Save the Panic Attack for Later

When you've just finished a dramatic or theatrical reading, don't wig out if the director or casting director asks you to do it again. Being redirected is a positive sign. It shows he or she is interested. Maybe this person wants to see how well you take direction. Or maybe he or she simply wants to see it done differently. Either reason is good and means your chances have just increased.

STRATEGY NO.

45

Don't Be a Sloppy Joe

Is your résumé updated? Are any of the credits written on it by hand? One of them scribbled on the page may be tolerable, but two or more look sloppy and imply a lack of caring. If you don't appear to care that much about yourself, how are you going to convince producers that you care about their project?

You can't concede defeat before you even start. If you are interested in acting ... just do it. Don't let anybody say you can't.

JAMES EARL JONES

STRATEGY NO.

46

Bring Your Back-Ups

This is a business, not a game. Don't forget to bring your picture and résumé with you to every reading—*including subsequent callbacks.* Even if you feel certain the casting director already has them from the first interview, you can never be absolutely certain. He or she is only human and can misplace things. Having an extra one on hand in just such an emergency reflects your professionalism.

STRATEGY NO.

47

Have Some Answers Ready

Every now and then during an interview, someone will pop the famous question, "So, how 'bout telling me a little about yourself?" If you want to score some points at this juncture, just be yourself and talk about things you're sincerely interested in. And don't dwell entirely upon acting. They know you're enthusiastic about the industry; otherwise you wouldn't be there. What they're truly interested in is your personality. What do you love to do in your spare time? Do you have an interesting job? Have you won awards or gained recognition in other fields outside of acting?

It will help to have a brief inventory ready in the back of your mind when you encounter this question. However, make certain you don't look as though you're reciting a list. Most important, endeavor to be brief; don't drone on and on.

The other question you may get is "What have you done lately?" It's an occasion for joy if you've just been wrapped from a recent project. But it's the pits if you haven't done anything for the last six months or more. The trick in this latter situation is to lead off your answer with the one key word that has mercifully allowed many an actor to get by. And that's "just." As in, "Well, I *just* finished a great show at Community Park Theater. I played 'Boots' in *A Gypsy's Tale*. We had a pretty good response. My character was a lot of fun, because … [and so on and so forth]." Even if you did the play in the summer and you're interviewing in the winter, the word "just" helps make it sound more immediate. The only drawback is if your last job was on a TV series that was cancelled three or four years ago. In that case, using this technique will date you, because the casting community stays abreast of that kind of information. However, if that's truly your situation, just make sure to have a persuasive reason for your absence from the industry.

Don't hesitate to give acting all you've got. If it's worth doing, it's worth doing right.

BETTE DAVIS

STRATEGY NO.

48

Develop the Knack of Implied Attire

Regarding the old argument of dressing for the part, you can be sure of one thing: lots of different people will give you lots of different advice. In the face of that, you can rely on one fact: most theatrical (i.e., film and TV) casting directors prefer you dress merely to *suggest* the role you're going out for. Dressing up right on the money—like a cop, for example—can do more damage than good. Walking in wearing a uniform or a police officer's hat conveys how desperately you want the job, and that suggests a lack of self-assurance. Entering in solid-color, dark clothing is a far more confident-looking and professional approach. (Don't forget Strategy no. 5!)

The same holds true for props. Casting directors would prefer that you mime, holding an imaginary tool or gun, rather than haul things into the room. And nowadays, bringing even a toy gun to your audition is unwise.

There is one vital exception, however, with respect to both wardrobe and props. When auditioning for a commercial, it's actually expected you'll dress right on the money—and even bring in a prop or two. And many actors will, going to elaborate extremes just to gain a competitive advantage.

Crazy business, isn't it?

STRATEGY NO.

49

Instill in Yourself a Clearly Defined Mood before Your Entrance

Whether you're aware of it or not, in most cases you'll start being evaluated the moment you walk through the door. Thus, the whole casting process begins well before you've even had a chance to show what you've prepared.

Just seeing you initiates the casting committee's selection process as they try to ascertain whether or not you meet all their expectations of the character. Therefore, it's a smart bet to come in with your character's nature already entrenched and readily apparent.

For example, if your role is quite solemn or even villainous, it doesn't do you the least bit of good to bounce into the room with a hearty handshake and a "damned-glad-to-be-here" look on your face. On the other hand, you don't want to appear so utterly gloomy they'll think you're on a day pass from the state hospital.

It's not about going overboard; it's about learning to temper your pre-reading interview demeanor through your character. And most critically, it's about learning to have it firmly on display before taking one step into the room.

I still, and always will, find it difficult at times to trust myself. It is seldom that I think I've been guilty of underacting. When I'm wrong, or off, it will usually be because I've done too much.

JACK LEMMON

STRATEGY NO.

50

Make Sure Your Questions Are Warranted

Quite often casting directors or directors themselves will ask if you have any questions before you begin your reading. If you have a legitimate question, then by all means, ask it. If you don't, and you're just attempting to be more engaging during your interview, then you're digging a hole. They can usually tell when you're doing that. And frankly, it turns them off.

If, on the other hand, you're genuinely cloudy about the nature of your character or unsure about a peculiar name or phrase, then you should indeed ask for clarification. It's an accepted practice. However, it pays to get as much information as possible cleared up *before* seeing the casting director, so the questions you do pose are substantive and therefore warranted.

STRATEGY NO.

51

Reprise the Wardrobe

If you find yourself in the callbacks, should you really dress exactly the same as you did for your first reading?

You bet! The casting people not only liked your talent, they liked the whole package. Oblige them once again by dressing the same way.

Acting is best enjoyed when we're unaware of technique.
LAURA DERN

STRATEGY NO.

52

The Squeaky Wheel Gets the Grease

From time to time, you'll be asked to read for a different part than the one you prepared for. This will happen either when you first arrive at the casting session or after your initial reading, and it means the director or producer feels you may be more suitable for another role. Either way, never be hesitant to clearly ask for adequate time to look over and prepare the new material. It would be very unusual for a producer or director not to grant you that courtesy.

STRATEGY NO.

53

Go for It!

Should you try out for industrial or student films? Certainly! You should go out for anything you have time for. While the better money naturally lies in the bigger, more conventional projects, getting more experience on smaller ones is an unbeatable way to learn your craft. Making mistakes on a student or small industrial film is far less costly than making them on a multimillion-dollar set. Consequently, there's far less stress. You can better acquire technical acting skills when you don't have the added pressures of a big-budget shoot.

I didn't start acting to be a movie star. I started in the theater and my desire was to get better at my craft. It's still my desire. Whatever labels people give me, that's not me or part of my craft. Come and talk to me on my fiftieth birthday and I may feel differently, but now, I'm just taking the lesson from one of my teachers who said, "Don't be afraid to fail big."

DENZEL WASHINGTON

STRATEGY NO.

54

Make Sure Your Photo Is Truly Representative

Your head shot is your calling card and all-important entrée to the business. The composition, the lighting, and the overall professionalism the shot reflects can make the difference in your being called in or not. Because of its obvious importance, you might be tempted to shoot for an exaggerated, glitzy effect, neglecting the highest priority of all: *you must look like the person in the photo* when you walk through the door at casting sessions. That means the style and length of your hair should be the same. For men, this means facial hair as well.

Take serious note: this issue is one of the biggest continuing complaints of casting directors. They call you in for an interview based precisely on your appearance. It's your look that matches their idea of the character. But if you come into the office looking much different than the photograph, you have wasted their time.

A basic rule of thumb for photos is to avoid the drastically lit and blatantly shadowy head shot. Such murky effects invariably end up being more of a distortion than an accurate reflection of how you truly appear. So choose a photographer actually recommended by casting directors or agents—one who won't be prone to such extreme practices. If, after you get your eight-by-ten done, you decide to cut your hair or substantially change the style, make another appointment right away to get new shots done.

When it comes to touching up photos, be very cautious. If the touch-up work is for some minute detail (such as digitizing out some odd, flyaway hair or compensating for a weird shadow), then you can certainly get away with it. However, far too many actors mistakenly allow computer artists a heavy hand if it makes their head shot more glamorous looking. They allow the artist to remove under-eye bags, scars, blotches, and far too many facial lines. The trouble with a lot of touch-up work is that it looks exactly like that: a lot of touch-up work—especially when you're standing in the audition room. When industry professionals see the comparison, believe me, they're not happy.

Women, when you pose for your head shots, make sure you do not rest the top of your hand directly underneath your chin. Nothing looks more affected and entirely amateurish than that. The actress in your photo should look like a person of confidence and professionalism, not a blushing bride. Your best choice is to keep your hands off your face, period. Don't let a photographer tell you otherwise.

When finally choosing your photo, don't let your non-industry friends or your mother help you decide. They're not involved in the entertainment field, so they tend to pick the glittery, pretentious ones. These kinds of pictures may stroke your ego or dazzle your family, but they'll rarely impress the people who really count.

Best bet: let your agent decide. Your agent knows you and knows the marketplace. Consequently, he or she will pick the type of head shot that stands a better chance of selling you. (Have another look at Strategy no. 34.)

STRATEGY NO.

55

To Stand or Not to Stand

Casting directors sometimes ask whether you prefer to stand or sit during an audition. The answer is stand. You convey more energy while standing than sitting. However, if you've been sitting during the interview, with your sides in your lap, and they ask you to begin your reading, there's no need to leap up out of your chair. That looks too eager. Merely begin from your seated position. (Review Strategy no. 5. In fact, why don't you put it up on your refrigerator today?)

Most directors just want you to ... be yourself in front of a camera.

KATHY BATES

STRATEGY NO.

56

Keep Your Modeling Career in the Background

Although you might be fortunate enough to be doing print work or ramp modeling, it can work against you if you let casting people know. Most of them have seen so many stiff models trying to act, they're convinced the majority can't. Unfortunately, that's true in far too many cases. But if you've been paying your dues and diligently studying your craft, you've got a good, fighting chance to disprove this common assumption.

Just keep your modeling info hush-hush for now. If you've got those kinds of credits on your résumé, you'd better remove them. Pronto.

STRATEGY NO.

57

Don't Be Rude and Intrude

If you think it's fun or beneficial to crash auditions, you're in for a surprise. You could get grounded before you're truly up and flying.

Perhaps you've heard of a few actors getting away with attending auditions they weren't scheduled for, but nearly every casting director will tell you not to do it. At the very least, it plays havoc with their schedules. If you find out there's something being cast that you're right for, call your agent and see if he or she can get you in.

If you ever decide to risk crashing a session, you'd better have two things going for you. One, you'd better be absolutely, physically right for the part. Two, you'd better be prepared to give one of the best readings of your life. Anything less could cost you dearly.

Always make your own decisions; never compromise your integrity, don't communicate unless you yourself want to communicate. I think living life, you have to rub elbows with all sorts of people. You have to be willing to experience anything. And if you live by those things, you're going to have a shot at a better life than you would normally.

JOHN TRAVOLTA

STRATEGY NO.

58

A Trick for Dyslexic Readers

If you're challenged with dyslexia, get your script or sides as far in advance as possible and memorize the scene. During the audition, hold your script up as you normally would during a cold reading in case you absolutely have to look down at one of your lines. (Since there's no script supervisor present, how else would you get a line if you forgot one?) You want to look as though you're cold-reading just like everybody else.

Hey, if Tom Cruise overcame it, so can you!

STRATEGY NO.

59

Use Your Nerves or Your Nerves Will Use You

Every actor at one time or another is overwhelmed by heart-pounding fear during an audition. Whether you're vying for a huge commercial contract or performing in front of a network panel of TV executives, there are always ample opportunities for stage-fright demons to sneak up on you.

You can help yourself immeasurably by recognizing performance panic for what it really is: wanting so badly to do the job flawlessly that you've mercilessly left yourself no room for error. That's all. However, allowing yourself a little kindness—giving yourself permission to make a mistake—can go a long way toward helping you overcome the anxiety.

Remember, making a mistake doesn't equal not getting the job. The people watching you know the stakes are high, and, believe it or not, they aren't turned off by a flubbed line or a stumble. They pay far more attention to your behavior than to the words.

Besides, there's a surprising advantage to having the jitters. Naturally, too much jitteriness can nearly render you useless. But a moderate amount generates a beneficial lift of energy. It provides a fascinating edge to your reading that otherwise might not be there. So keep that positive aspect of nervousness in mind, prepare to make a mistake or two, and leave the rest to the unfolding moments of the reading.

If you can recognize nervousness for what it is, you can use it for what it can be. If you don't, expect it to forever hold you back.

If you put pressure on yourself, that's when you shut down and get afraid. You need to take risks.
ELIZABETH SHUE

STRATEGY NO.

60

Avoid the Big No-No

Even though you might presently be doing extra work or have done it in the past, never put down "extra" credits (background work) on your résumé! You'll end up losing major points. You're at an audition to convince the casting committee that you're a principal performer, not a human prop.

There's an unspoken stigma attached to atmosphere work. Even though you might be doing it temporarily with sincere aspirations to speaking roles, the industry still has a rigid tendency to lump you together with all the other "professional extras" (the ones going nowhere in the industry except back and forth in backgrounds).

Another taboo is listing your "extra" work in major TV series or films in such a way as to make it look as though you had a speaking part. For various reasons, casting directors can usually spot that ruse. Not only that, you'll have a lot of explaining to do if you wind up auditioning for the person who actually directed one of those projects.

STRATEGY NO.

61

Prepare for Adventures in Happy Land

You've watched enough TV commercials to know that the majority of them feature happy, "up" people all the time. This is definitely not the place for the sullen, smoldering look you've been practicing for your film close-ups.

This is Happy Land, and its extremely animated citizens are thrilled to be using miraculous products to solve dreadful problems and magically improve life. Sometimes watching people get ecstatic over frozen waffles or shampoo may strain your credulity a bit, but that's what commercial producers want: actors who come across as enthusiastic, bubbly, and full of life. Exuberance sells the product, and, most important, it sells you. It's safe to say that in the audition room, you can never have enough of it.

Strip your work of affectations. Play for realism. Play without fear, without caution.

SIR JOHN GIELGUD

STRATEGY NO.

62

Have Another Choice in Your Hip Pocket

You may ask the director his or her point of view in order to confirm the choices you've so carefully made for your character. But if you do, you'd better be ready for some curve balls. For instance, what you may have confidently interpreted as lively and genuine warmth on the part of your character may turn out to be a facade for guilt. It's not uncommon for directors to give you just such an opposing view. Some chatty directors will even volunteer shockingly new information without your asking. In any event, if you don't have an alternate way of playing the scene, you could be sunk.

The reason for such unexpected particulars is that by the time you get to the audition, the director has carefully analyzed the script from front to back. But you've never even seen it. All you've had to go on were a few pages sliced out from somewhere between the first page and the last. So you can be faced with the challenge of giving a performance reflecting the director's views about the character just seconds after learning what they are.

As any experienced actor will tell you, it's not a simple matter to instantly change a scene from the way you've been rehearsing it over and over. You've got to overcome emotions and behavior patterns you've continually reinforced.

To avoid becoming too entrenched, it's best to rehearse your audition scene in as many different ways as time will allow. Naturally, you'll adopt certain choices as your favorite ones, but make sure you're absolutely comfortable doing your scene at least two very different ways. That way, if you're forced to change emotional gears, you'll have a far greater chance of success. Instead of trying on the spot to frantically alter or even reverse the familiar patterns you established earlier, you'll glide into the new adjustments with a comfortable sense of déjà vu.

STRATEGY NO.

63

Center Yourself

If you wanted to distill all the components of acting down to the simplest of terms, it would be this: acting is 90 percent anxiety management and only 10 percent technique. If you want to be at your absolute best (and who doesn't?), it's imperative that you quiet your straying thoughts and achieve a state of "centeredness" just prior to your reading time.

Many different actors have their own method. Slow, deep breathing is one. Meditating is another. Even doing push-ups is a popular means with some actors. Over time, you'll discover through trial and error what's best for you.

You may well find that among many methods, nothing quite helps as much as that peaceful sense of complete self-assurance that arises from thorough preparation beforehand. That is, all the analysis you could do was done, and all the ways you could play it were explored. After that, add a method of relaxation when you arrive to serve as a finishing touch that will help to eliminate most of the inevitable butterflies.

I've just learned how to do this acting thing. All the rest of my work before was just one, big acting lesson. I do it now from a place of joy.

JESSICA LANGE

STRATEGY NO.

64

Don't Say You Can If You Can't

A sure-fire method of getting on the bad side of a director is eagerly claiming to possess a specific skill you don't have. You can blackball yourself from any further work with that director, or even the entire production company, by showing up on the day of the shoot and clumsily attempting to ice skate or ride a horse.

If you have a reasonable expectation that you can perform a certain skill because you have some previous experience with it—even if it's just a little—that's fair. Tell the people in the audition you can do it. Then brush up or take lessons in the time remaining before your shoot date.

STRATEGY NO.

65

Keep the Million-Dollar Question in Mind

"What are they *really* looking for?" If you haven't already asked that classic question a number of times, you've probably heard other performers utter it ad infinitum.

You can practically numb yourself attending endless seminars seeking the varied answers. Or you can read countless books in an attempt to dig up more details. Actors with little experience ask that question all the time. But more established performers know the answer. And they can boil it down for you into two basic parts.

First off, the people who cast projects need to know whether the production personnel can get along with you. Are you cordial and affable? Are you amenable to change? This is the main reason for the short chit-chat session that precedes many readings. It's essentially a veiled ritual whose purpose is to determine your professionalism. Secondly, they want someone who not only fits the character description, but can most convincingly act out the part—in other words, a strong actor. Anything other than these two key factors is nothing more than the personal preferences of individual casting directors.

Moral of this story? You'll get farther, faster, by developing an easygoing but thoroughly professional attitude, conjoined to a constant refinement of your acting skills. Period. Incessantly trying to figure out or anticipate what each and every casting director looks for will make you a superb candidate for a straitjacket.

I don't know the key to success. But the key to failure is trying to please everybody.

BILL COSBY

STRATEGY NO.

66

Color Your World Wisely

Never overlook the psychological influences of color. Often disregarded because it's such a subtle concept, its judicious use can nevertheless provide you with a competitive edge.

As an example, if you're going in to audition for a criminal role, would it be prudent to wear pastel colors? Of course not! They're light hues that imply warmth and serenity. (Check out a dentist's office sometime.) By the same token, if you're going in to read for a "nice" part, like the role of a mother or father, then dark, sullen colors worn from head to toe would more than likely harm your chances.

STRATEGY NO.

67

Don't Just Pounce, Pronounce

When you look over your script or sides, make sure that you know the meaning and correct pronunciation of every word. Words are part and parcel of your craft, and mispronouncing unfamiliar ones in a presumptuous way during auditions does little beyond making you look ignorant. (If you don't think so, try doing it twice in one audition and see if you get the job.)

If you have the slightest doubt about a word or name, look up the pronunciation in the dictionary or ask someone. And remember, always ask *before* you go in to read. If you don't appear to have a good command of the language, your overall ability to perform may be suspect.

*I believe you have a responsibility to comport yourself
in a manner that gives an example to others. As a young
man, I prayed for success. Now I pray just to be worthy
of it.*

BRENDAN FRASER

STRATEGY NO.

68

Know What You're Selling

Anyone in the field of sales will readily tell you that in order to get more business, you have to know your product inside and out.

What this means for you is that it's a waste of time and energy to spend untold hours poring over your script in order to get an increasingly better sense of your character. Your character isn't the real product. It's best in the long run to simply be yourself. Believe it or not, that's what most casting directors are actually looking for.

Day in and day out, casting directors see actors playing it safe, adhering fanatically to how they believe the character should behave. Often, how the character behaves is also obvious to all the other actors vying for the same role. If nearly everyone comes in and does practically the same thing, who do you think will stand out?

Make no mistake: a little character research is helpful. It leads you to suppress some things and enhance others. But your personality, with all its unique quirks, good or bad, is infinitely more fascinating than a well-drawn but wholly predictable character. And that's what should always come through: you. It's your main product. The better you know it, the better it sells.

THE PERFORMANCE STRATEGIES

You've got two things to do in that audition room: Get the part, or be remembered.

RICHARD DREYFUS

STRATEGY NO.

69

Lose the Room and Do the Take

Your effectiveness in an audition rises and falls on one word: concentration. Distractions, whether external or internal, are costly. Let your focus, therefore, be so strong that you form a mental canopy that excludes everything around you except the objects of your attention—namely, the person or persons you're reading with.

Take this process a step further by actually imagining yourself doing a take rather than an audition. It's a great way to ensure your concentration will be unusually keen, helping you to look more authentic in an artificial environment.

STRATEGY NO.

70

Lower Your Horns and Keep Charging

If you stumble over a word during a reading, it's best to forget about it and keep forging ahead. While presumptuously mispronouncing a word will often cost you points, a common trip of the tongue will not. What could hurt you, though, is letting that verbal stumble upset you so much that you kick yourself mentally as you continue to read. That kind of internal-dialogue performance monitoring instantly causes you to read in a distant-sounding, unconfident manner. Would *you* cast anybody who read like that?

I will never let myself get away with the phony.
ANNE BANCROFT

STRATEGY NO.

71

Above All Else, Aspire to Truth

Helen Hayes once said, "An actor's life is one, long search—a search to be more truthful in one's work." Her remark underscores the fact that being entirely convincing has long been the craft's most vital trait. In a manner of speaking, it's the one difference that can make all the difference. For when it comes time to audition, you can prepare all you want, you can analyze your scene over and over, and you can endlessly examine and dissect your character until it seems there's nothing else left to do. But no matter how much you've prepared, if the results aren't realistic, neither are your chances of success. That's why this is the most detailed of the 101 Strategies.

How can you harness truthfulness? How can you ensure the incomparable quality of utter realism will appear in all your performances?

To begin with, scene work often lacks complete plausibility when it's laden with excessive planning. All your well-intentioned efforts can mire you in inflexibility. It's only logical that the more you anticipate precisely what you're going to do in a scene, the more you'll be disinclined to do anything different. Some label this predicament "analysis paralysis."

Accomplished actors realize this and therefore endeavor to appear anything but bogged down with rigidly ingrained ideas. In short, they strive to react rather than to act. Through experience, they've come to appreciate the sparkle of the honest freshness and novelty that emerge when spontaneity is allowed to come into play.

Developing a genuine ability to react, therefore, is a top priority. Trusting more in your own gut responses than in a detailed, cerebral plan is a challenge worth your best efforts.

A reliable way to build this self-trust and achieve believable behavior is to focus on the *other* actor's behavior. Don't just act listening—actively listen. Listen to what your partner is saying, and, even more important, watch how he or she says it.

Paying that much concerted attention to the other person while you're acting has an uncanny effect. All at once, it erases the look of anticipation in your face. Any appearance of self-consciousness or rigidity disappears because you're primarily removing your attention from yourself. Instead of being burdened with the insecurity of what you're going to do next, you become more concerned with, and affected by, what you see. The more you see, the more you're affected. The more you're affected, the more you're genuinely responding. *That's* reacting.

Reactions demonstrate you're living authentically from actual, unforeseen circumstances developing in the scene—not out of preconceived notions as to how it all should fit. By allowing yourself to become so caught up in the other person's behavior, you have little time or tendency to consciously contrive your own.

Your subconscious is remarkably equipped to handle the whole situation quite well. Case in point: If you could sit behind a movie screen and look out at the members of the audience, you'd notice they certainly need no reminder to watch the screen. Nor are they scheming about how they're going to respond from one moment to the next. They're merely sitting there, so genuinely engrossed that they're reacting to everything, all without a single lesson in acting!

A very large part of all this is being open enough to recognize and allow more of what you haven't prepared for: unplanned feelings. Don't negate or attempt to bury any of them. Repressing your emotions leaves fleeting but unmistakable traces on your face. And that doesn't look truthful. Freely expressing those feelings, however, does.

Let's say you're going to do a sensitive scene. The other actor suddenly departs from your personal game plan, inspired to become more weepy than you'd counted on, or even hysterical, for that matter. You can't afford to deny that it's happening— that's how you start to look inflexible. Even though his or her unpredictable emotions weren't part of your personal preparation, if you don't want to look wooden, you have to instantly relate to them. You must concede to the presence of unanticipated feelings with your own corresponding vocal tones and behavior, which essentially announce, "I see, and I acknowledge." Anything else is a deadly form of denial.

You may have planned to carry out your scene with a sympathetic attitude and all the soft vocal tones that may accompany it. Yet, if your scene partner begins out of the blue to break down and sob, you're going to have to adapt or relate to it. You'll have to get even more sympathetic (maybe even put your arm around his or her shoulder). Or you can adopt a stern attitude of "come on, get hold of yourself." Plainly, what you cannot do is just remain the same, stuck in an idea from a previous moment, now past.

Don't forget, the same holds true for your own potential emotions. If, during this scene, you start to get impulses that make you a lot sadder than you thought you'd be, then, by all means, let those feelings surface.

The stronger the actor you work with, the more likely you are to see inspired departures like those in the example I've just described. Seasoned performers aren't afraid of departing from a preconceived plan because they've learned to welcome the unpredictable outcomes of inspired moments. They know that an actor who's unpredictable is not just convincing, but captivating.

To summarize, you're faced with a choice. You can either be in your head and perform a scene, or you can get out of your head to watch, listen, and live it. A scene that you really live doesn't contain one false note, because your outer, forward focus allows you to achieve a level of total involvement; you get caught up in the action, thoroughly believing everything that's going on. The direct result of that level of commitment is clear: when you believe everything that's going on in your scene, so does everyone watching it.

STRATEGY NO.

72

It Can't All Be Neil Simon

It's a given that you're going to come across material from time to time that you simply don't like. Whether it's the writing itself or the subject matter, eventually you're bound to run into a script you don't exactly relish.

Watch out for this trap. While you have every right to disagree with or even hate the material, one fact has to be faced: you must make an honest attempt to find something about it that you do like. Otherwise, your distaste for the material will emerge during your reading. And it's not even a conscious thing. You think you're going through another audition as usual, but somehow the distaste for the writing bleeds through. This prevents you from giving a solid, viscerally connected reading, and you end up with one that's dull and dispassionate.

To be a good actor, you've got to stay somewhere around eight years old. And you need confidence.

CHRISTOPHER WALKEN

STRATEGY NO.

73

Beware the Night of the Living Casting Directors

At nearly a third of all your auditions, you're going to encounter a "zombie" casting director. That's one who reads the other character's lines during your audition but gives you so little emotionally, you'd swear he or she didn't have a pulse. Maybe this person is tired from seeing scores of actors all day, or maybe he or she doesn't have an acting background and isn't familiar with the concept of providing you with something to feed off of. In any case, this person still expects you somehow to materialize a performance by some kind of mystical solo osmosis.

Obviously, auditioning in front of directors and producers with that kind of casting director as your scene partner can be a major disadvantage. He or she can get away with looking dead; you can't. The situation poses a dilemma. On one hand, you don't want to tune in to him or her the way you would with an experienced actor. You'll just get pulled down to the same fatally low energy level and appear equally boring. On the other hand, you certainly can't afford to compensate by summoning up fabricated feelings. That makes you look like you're overacting.

This predicament might sound discouraging, but there is an upside to it. Namely, you're on an even playing field. Everyone else reading for your role is getting the very same treatment. And fortunately, you can use a neat trick to make yourself stand out.

Prepare a clearly drawn, impassioned goal. Some actors refer to this as their "action" or "objective." In any case, it's a result you ardently wish to see acknowledged in the casting director's behavior during your reading. (Ultimately, it's what your character wants as well. You're just focusing on the casting director personally as opposed to acting to another character.)

While the reading is underway, this prearranged response you struggle to get out of the casting director will naturally be thwarted by his or her sheer indifference. As an immediate result, it will generate within you one of two completely genuine feelings: mounting frustration or increasing amusement.

Let's say you're reading for the part of a crooked business-person trying to get a reluctant associate to agree to a shady plan. Knowing you're going to be seeing a lifeless casting director, you formulate a strong, uncomplicated goal, such as demanding obedience from the other character. As the reading gets under way, you begin to see the casting director exhibiting anything but obedient behavior or compliant tones. Not getting what you want, therefore, should be a frustrating experience, stimulating you to work harder in order to succeed.

These rising sensations serve to increase your performance energy in safe, incremental levels. What's more, they come out as they're supposed to: realistically. That's because they're arising authentically out of the interaction between you and the casting director, not artificially, out of your head. It's an example of the time-tested wisdom that good acting is reacting.

The only decision you have to make after formulating your goal is which feeling to play to. That's easy enough. If the scene is of a confrontational nature (as in the example just described), let the frustrations come through. If the scene is of a happier nature, then let the arising amusement come up and color your work.

At this point you may ask, "How do I know whether the casting director I'm going to read with will give me such apathetic treat-ment in the first place?" The truth is, you don't—unless you already know the person. But here's some unbeatable advice: just as every fighter pilot carries a packed parachute for all mis-sions, every actor should carry a passionate objective for all audition scenes. It's better to have it and not need it than to need it and not have it.

STRATEGY NO.

74

Avoid the King Kong Approach

You may have a scene in which the opportunity arises for you to get into quite an emotional uproar. Have enough presence of mind, however, not to pound on the walls or pick up something and hurl it across the room. This may seem obvious, but it's well worth noting, because these things sometimes happen in the heat of the moment. When it does, you can generally count on one thing: being counted out. The casting committee will think you're a little on the wild side and liable to get out of control.

Eliminate the obvious and keep it simple.

MARY STEENBURGEN

STRATEGY NO.

75

Practice Saying Your Name

Your character's name, that is. Sometimes you'll have a scene in which you have to introduce yourself to other characters. For example, "I'm Special Agent Franklin Simmons (or Special Agent Patricia Wells), Federal Bureau of Investigation."

Make sure you read that self-introducing line far more times than all the other ones. By the time you audition, you want your name and what you do to roll off your tongue as if you've said it a thousand times before. After all, in your character's world, he or she has. Tripping over your own character's name or hesitating about your character's vocation looks and sounds dreadfully weak.

STRATEGY NO.

76

Trust in the Economy of Motion

If you've been to a fair number of commercial auditions, you've discovered that moving around in your scene is usually expected. For example, you'll be directed to pantomime an activity such as lifting a phantom cup of coffee or opening and shutting an unseen door. All this is part of the effort to eventually bring attention to the real star: the product.

Because movement plays such an important role in on-camera salesmanship, sometimes there's confusion as to whether to bring it into the dramatic arena. That is, should you or shouldn't you move around while auditioning for a TV series or a film as opposed to a commercial?

The good new is, you don't have to do much at all. Casting directors have seen plenty of "cups" or "weapons" suddenly "dropped" or "closed doors" forgotten about. Needless to say, that can make a dramatic scene look pretty hokey.

Most film directors aren't that concerned about blocking. They know they can work out the stage movements later with the actual props on hand. What they're really interested in seeing is whether you can interpret the material and make it look emotionally realistic, not whether you can demonstrate all the physicalities. So if you have some action indicated by the script, trust in doing as little as possible and concentrate more on your emotional investment.

As an example, what you say before or after you fire a make-believe gun will have more impact if it's said with utter conviction, with minimal attention given to the weapon. Just holding up your fist is sufficient. Don't go overboard and make an issue out of blowing smoke, pretending to load it, and so on. Convincing work comes more from the heart than the hand. If your words are impassioned and unimpeachably honest, you need little else.

Method? Shit! Just show me which button to push.

JASON ROBARDS

STRATEGY NO.

77

Stay Focused During Your "Pre-Game" Period

Use your time wisely in the waiting room by centering yourself or getting clear on your objectives. Even if you feel totally prepared, it won't hurt to concentrate on your "moment before" (the imaginary action or dialogue preceding the actual scene).

It's a waste of precious time to sit around socializing with the rest of the actors in the room. Chit-chat does nothing for you but dangerously scatter your much-needed attention and energy. There's enough time for talking outside the office or studio after the reading.

STRATEGY NO.

78

Maximize the Conflict

The great director Alfred Hitchcock used to say that drama was life with the dull bits cut out. When you think of all the things that can challenge characters in the brief time frame of a feature film or an episode of a TV series, it's hard to disagree.

Those challenges are moments that make any production worth watching. They come from the way the writer uses the most important element in any story: conflict. Well-conceived conflict nearly always results in good plots.

Strong auditions are marked by conflict as well. Anytime your character has a goal or expectation thwarted, you have conflict.

So if you get to audition in just such a confrontational scene, consider yourself lucky. It's your chance to shine—if you play it to the hilt.

The maximizing process is relatively simple. You can achieve it by exaggerating the consequences of the conflict. Some like to call this "raising the stakes." This means formulating your motivation into more of a life-or-death issue. And all that takes is a little drastic language.

Let's say you have a scene where your life partner's love for you is in question. Consequently, the intent or subtext you might've created underneath your dialogue goes something like, "I need you to want me." That might be something worth fighting for in your scene, but it'll hardly come out looking like a championship slugfest in the audition room, where it counts most. However, you can intensify the same core issue by restating it in more desperate terms. Your new intent, rephrased, can go something like, "If I don't have your love, I'll end my life."

Like any new skill, this will take a little practice at first, but it's worth it. You'll find that maximizing the conflict instantly unleashes more intense and realistic feelings than all the prearranged transitions you could possibly structure into a scene.

The training I have is in my brain and it works on material in not-so-conscious ways. I have all sorts of complicated, computerized knowledge stored away in the back of my mind. When I do then wing it, a lot of work has been done that I wouldn't have time to sit down and explain to everybody.

GERALDINE PAGE

STRATEGY NO.

79

Improve Your Improv

It's fair to say that over half the commercials you'll audition for will require improvisation in one form or another. Consequently, developing strong improv skills will enable you to enjoy an enormous advantage.

This kind of acting is often misunderstood or taken for granted as just a spur-of-the-moment routine of "winging it"—that is, spontaneously saying whatever comes up within the context of your character. While that may be the fundamental premise, it's far from being the whole ball game. Successful improvisation depends primarily upon the nonstop, unbroken flow of discussion or activity that constantly takes place between the performers. An improvised scene will collapse if stalled by hesitancy or unmotivated silence.

Anything you do or say during an improv must not be self-centered, but rather must be something that acknowledges the other actor's last line. That keeps the flow of performance energy moving and alive. A few basic rules will keep an improvised scene streaming along nicely.

1. *Never ask questions.* You can cause a delay in another performer's flow by asking something he or she has to think about for a couple of seconds in order to respond.

2. *Never deny.* If someone in your scene declares something absurd, such as that they've just landed on Earth from another planet, never say, "No, you didn't. I can tell you're a human." That can break the rapid flow between the two of you by forcing the other actor to mentally regroup in awkward silence in order to try another angle.

3. *Always build.* This is the logical extension of the other two rules. For instance, if your partner declares he or she has just landed here from another planet, you can build upon it by adding something like, "Yes, I can tell. You have that fresh, just-landed look."

Remember these three vital rules. And better still, take one or two improvisation workshops to really get the knack. The next time you're in a commercial audition requiring something improvised, you'll be thankful you did.

STRATEGY NO.

80

Cultivate Presence

You've no doubt heard the remark, "That actor has presence." Russell Crowe has lots of it. Barbara Streisand has plenty. And Tommy Lee Jones has it in spades.

You might believe that presence is a result of a person's fame. It might be more accurate to say that fame is a result of presence. But no matter how you view it, you can't afford to be without it.

Stripped of any pomp or pretense, this appealing quality amounts to not much more than a serene temperament born out of ample self-assurance. And you'll start to exhibit more of it in your own auditions if you make this Strategy an unwavering practice.

Firstly, approach your roles with a sense of ownership, as if the part were actually written for you. In a way, that's not far from the truth. You're already the character by virtue of being deemed, because of your picture, physically right for the part. You must walk in thoroughly convinced of that fact. You must already own the role.

Never give up your ownership. Even if you feel the casting director is off base—if you genuinely know you're not quite suitable for the part—then you must make up your mind to give such a strong, turn-your-guts-inside-out performance that you'll make those watching you honestly consider rewriting the character.

Secondly, back up your belief in ownership with a supreme sense of conviction within your upcoming scene. Use what you firmly believe to be the absolute best of all possible motivations or objectives. There's no room for doubt. It's got to be the greatest one.

Using this two-part tactic in your auditions will cause you to exude a commanding influence all around the room. No one will fail to pick up on your attitude of certitude or self-assurance. More to the point, you'll enjoy the kinds of results your competition considers to be reserved for the big guns.

Acting is not acting. It is an art form which must appear artless. If I see someone "working at it," I lose interest.
TONY CURTIS

STRATEGY NO.

81

Wager on the Middle Ground

A producer who frequently attends casting sessions remarked to me that as far as he was concerned, there were only three auditioning styles. He said actors performed like either trees, space cadets, or humans.

He explained that "trees" come in so overly prepared, they cannot convincingly respond to any stimuli. They're wooden. There's just no reacting in their acting.

"Space cadets," on the other hand, believe passionately in the power of inspiration alone. They throw preparation out the window and wing their way through their scenes, often giving readings wildly out of context with the scene's design.

"Humans," however, stand on the middle ground. They are thoroughly prepared, well aware of the scene's intent, yet fully open to inspiration and instant change. As a result, they appear far more realistic.

This one producer's definitive observation leaves little doubt as to which approach yields your best odds.

STRATEGY NO.

82

Never Forget That Speed Kills

Anxiety has an unfortunately nasty way of rushing your reading. It causes you to speak faster than normal, serving only to suppress the emotional life of your scene. Feelings don't have time to grow and flourish if you're zipping along like an auctioneer.

Another primary cause of hasty readings is excessive concern about your timing—being trigger-happy. For instance, just as the casting director finishes his or her last line, you jump on his or her last breath or syllable with the beginning of your own line, all in an attempt to effect the sense of a timely response. This looks forced. People watching that sort of exchange don't get the benefit of a second or two to digest what's being said between the two characters. If they don't have the opportunity to assimilate what's going on, how can you appear to be doing so? There's nothing very realistic or sincere about contriving a quick response to something you didn't quite hear.

Remember, there's no sin in taking your time when auditioning. As a matter of fact, you're better off erring on the side of slowness. At the very least, during an unhurried reading you'll be better able to listen to the other lines and take in more of what's actually going on in the scene. As a result, you'll look far more connected.

If you look slow and yet connected, all a director has to think about is telling you to pick up your pace. If you look disconnected and fast, all a director will be thinking is "Who's next?"

After all these years, I'm still in the process of self-discovery. It's better to explore life and make mistakes than to play it safe. Mistakes are part of the dues one pays for a full life.

SOPHIA LOREN

STRATEGY NO.

83

Love Your Auditions

Treat every audition as another opportunity to plunge joyfully into your craft. Why? Because going in to land a job never has as favorable an outcome as going in to have a good time.

View your readings exactly as if they were limited-engagement, one-act performances that you do for the people in the audition room. Once done, you take an "inner bow" by thanking them and then promptly make your exit. This approach will definitely charge your work with a more energetic, committed quality—one that often places you a notch higher on the shelf of possible picks.

STRATEGY NO.

84

Play for Possibilities, Not Results

One of the great challenges in the audition room is to display enough motivation to appear interesting or passionate, but not so much as to appear overly prepared or overboard. Overboard means it looks like you're trying too hard. Overly prepared always looks stiff. And both look anything but helpful. (Remember Strategy no. 5? Is it on your refrigerator yet?)

You can begin to establish a sense of proper emotional proportion by first trusting that your homework will always come through. And it generally does so with less effort than most performers imagine. In fact, many actors attach so much importance to motivation that they treat it as if getting the role were based on this skill alone.

You don't need to get caught up in overtly and repeatedly broadcasting your choices through every mannerism and line of dialogue just so your auditioners get it. By the time you've spoken your second line, your motivation or intention has been displayed clearly through your demeanor and thus, in a sense, has been fulfilled. At that point, you can consciously let it recede so you can pay more attention to what impact your motivation is having on your scene partner. This will allow you to become absorbed in a far more creative moment-to-moment exchange, enabling you to add those all-important instinctive touches—the possibilities.

When the compelling dimension of fluid instincts appears in your work, you effectively eliminate every trace of restrictive preplanning and, more important, the harmful appearance of trying too hard.

Something happened with me. It was like a monkey off my back or something. I didn't feel armored any longer as an actor; I felt like I could—whatever I did—was going to be alright. It was a beginning for me, of a kind of subconscious work.

GENE HACKMAN

STRATEGY NO.

85

Reserve a Return-Trip Ticket

Once in a while, you'll be called in for a part that you're certain just isn't you. The character is so far removed from your look, age, and personality that auditioning will make you feel out of place, and you have little hope of success. However, don't give in to feelings of resignation and just end up "phoning your lines in."

There are two very good reasons for not giving up. The first is that the casting director might be thinking of changing the attributes of the character more in your direction. The second is that you should always give an audition your absolute best. Even if you're not picked for the role, a strong or memorable performance practically secures a return visit in the future to that same casting director.

STRATEGY NO.

86

Watch Those Hands

Don't touch casting directors during a reading. Forgive the pun, but they are indeed touchy about this. This is because they don't know how far you're going to go, especially if they sense the possibility that you could get carried away.

There is one exception, however. If you think a certain amount of contact is absolutely crucial to the scene, talk it over with the casting director sometime before the actual reading and get his or her permission. The courtesy will be appreciated.

We all try to put our best foot forward in front of people, but as an actor, your flaws are your gold. Your weaknesses and less-than-perfect parts are your most interesting.

HELEN HUNT

STRATEGY NO.

87

Start Strong, Finish Strong

Your ability to leave a lasting impression with your reading is predicated not only on how strongly you finish, but on how strongly you start. You can accomplish this by memorizing the first and last lines of your audition scene. That way, you can begin with your eyes and full mental focus on the other reader and end in the very same way.

It's definitely to your advantage, however, not to go to extremes—to actually memorize *all* your lines in long and complicated scenes. (It's okay to memorize short scenes and commercials.) For one thing, you can get carried away emotionally, which is highly desirable, and forget a line or two, which isn't so desirable. At that point, who's going to give you your line if you need it? The casting director? Maybe, but that's going to cost you a lot of points. Taking time to recover your dialogue and regain your feelings often results in a disastrous plunge in energy and confidence, no matter how well you started out.

The other hazard to memorized auditions is the not uncommon practice of casting directors notifying you when you arrive that some of your scenes have been rewritten or cut out entirely. But if all you've done is memorize your beginnings and endings, you've not wasted any time, and, furthermore, you'll adjust better to these kinds of abrupt changes.

One last item about memorizing your audition scenes: When the people who bring you in watch you work without a script, they sometimes presume unfairly that this is the best you can do with the scene. However, when they see you still working with your sides, they imagine there's still some untapped potential.

STRATEGY NO.

88

Gaze Deep into the Crystal Eye

Once in a while, you'll have to audition by reading directly into a camera. The best advice is not to consider it a camera at all. Peer right into the middle of the lens and picture a real person in your life—someone you love (or hate, if the scene calls for it)—and speak personally to that individual.

This indispensable technique guarantees your audition will be imbued with connection and realism, free of the artificial mannerisms that come from trying to relate to a lifeless device.

I like to think of myself as the Pete Rose of actors. Pete Rose wasn't the most talented athlete, but he made up for it with hustle. I sold suits, insurance, drew caricatures at a mall, sold women's shoes, stumbled through a million things and ended up on a movie set because someone said, "You really ought to give acting a shot." The only failure I know is never making the attempt.

GEORGE CLOONEY

STRATEGY NO.

89

Zero In on the Writer's Intent

Knowing the writer's intent nowadays is as vital to your audition as being able to speak. So many producers and directors are currently writers themselves that you can usually count on the person who either wrote your script or collaborated on it to be present at your audition. If you make the right choices, playing your part close to what the writer has in mind, your chances of landing the part will increase. To profit consistently from this, it's important to begin with a little background on the nature of dramatic writing.

Classic, three-act story structure has a prevailing current that continuously flows forward. Each scene, in its own individual way, fits into this flow, leading inevitably to the conclusion.

The characters that inhabit the story cannot escape their duty to serve this literary principle. They continually say and do things to advance all their scenes in the direction of the finale. And herein lies the sum and substance of this Strategy: the characters' words and actions are entirely dependent upon their desires. They speak only because they either want something or are responding to others who want something. (Confirm that for yourself by critically watching any film or TV series episode.) The writer's need or intent to keep the story moving is therefore identical to his or her characters' needs to fulfill their desires. Pinpoint your character's foremost desire in your audition scene and you've made one of the strongest choices possible.

Let's look at a hypothetical scene where a man and woman are having an argument. She strongly suspects him of being unfaithful and is telling him to pack his bags. He's trying to tell her it's all a misunderstanding.

This isn't just a yelling contest. Both characters have a need. Her need is that she feels the relationship is over and wants him to leave. His is that he believes in continuing the relationship and wants to remain. His desire clashes with hers, and the result is a sense of conflict, of rising urgency. Inevitably, this all leads to a climax and, ultimately, to a finish.

Uncover exactly what your character wants and you can use that as your choice, playing it through the dialogue in your scene. A genuine sense of urgency will naturally come through, without your having to push it. Why? The words will push it for you. Your impulses will do the rest. Trusting in that process makes for some excellent film acting and brings you closer to getting the role.

An example comes from Jack Nicholson. An actor who worked with him told me the Academy Award–winning actor admitted he liked using this approach in his work. He begins his scenes with a definite need in mind. If he gets what he wants, he's happy, and a sense of cheerfulness crops up in his dialogue. If, on the other hand, he doesn't get what he wants, it makes him moody or cranky, and that comes through in his responses as well. In any event, he allows for enough creative flexibility to surprise even himself, thereby achieving the best of both worlds: he takes advantage of the augmenting effect of the writer's intent but remains open to impulses that fuel his well-known spontaneity.

(Special note: You may have noticed this Strategy is very similar to Strategy no. 73. The difference between the two is that in this Strategy, you play out your objective more or less as planned. In Strategy no. 73, you decide in advance which side of the objective you'll play—amused or frustrated.)

STRATEGY NO.

90

Settle In to Settle Down

If you think that giving scattered, anxiety-ridden readings is somehow a brilliant way to audition, be sure to arrive only moments before your scheduled appointment. Nothing can upset your sense of well-being and confidence more than rushing from the parking lot into the building and right into the audition room.

Strive to get to the studio or office a bit earlier than necessary. This goes a long way toward helping you settle in and shake off the day, which lets you get more centered and focus effectively on your pending read. This, incidentally, offers the additional bonus of allowing you further preparation time in the event that lines have been rewritten or suddenly you're asked to read for an altogether different part.

Give yourself permission to succeed, and don't let fear bring you down. Fear is not a natural state of being; it's a decision you make. People say, You can't do it." But that's their game, their opinion, and it doesn't necessarily have anything to do with who you are or what you can do.

VIRGINIA MADSEN

STRATEGY NO.

91

Read the Fine Print

Regardless of how confident you feel after preparing for a reading, make doubly sure you've covered every square centimeter of your sides. Sometimes, during the first or second read-through, it's easy to miss a physical action cue (or blocking) that's buried between the lines of dialogue with the other characters. For instance, you may have a few words of direction indicating that you look over your shoulder before saying your line. Or you may have directions to stand or sit somewhere during the scene. Or you could be required to hand something to or take something from your scene partner or the casting director. If you miss those kinds of physical cues, you can be caught embarrassingly unaware when the other person carries out his or her half of the blocking responsibilities. Your sudden surprise and resulting awkwardness practically obliterate everything that went well before that point.

STRATEGY NO.

92

How to Face the Toughest Audition of All

Without a doubt, the toughest audition you'll ever face is the one that leads to all the others: auditioning for an agent. You won't get very far in the industry without one. So trying out for an agent in his or her office or performing for one at a showcase can make you go pretty rubbery in the knees. It's not often that so much is riding on your performance.

If you're lucky, you might be in a play good enough for you to feel comfortable inviting your potential representative to come and watch. Even so, many savvy agents will still prefer to have you read TV or film sides right in front of them, in an office, before they take you on. An encounter that is up close and personal gives them an idea of how truthful and contained you're likely to appear when you audition for on-camera parts.

If an agent asks you to do a monologue, you may want to consider looking for someone else, unless you're interested only in theater. A monologue is more of a stage device, and you won't find any TV casting directors in this part of the galaxy who even request it anymore. The talent buyers in the industry want to see and hear dialogue—and dialogue performed naturally. You should be wary of any agent who seems unaware of this and asks you to do a monologue. If the agent you're auditioning for has a good reputation for getting his or her clients work and still insists on a monologue, you may want to oblige. But if you have any hesitation about performing one, you don't have to. There's another option.

You can immediately put yourself in the driver's seat and increase your chances of representation by making a simple suggestion. It's best to pose it in the diplomatic form of an honest question. Just ask if the agent would mind your performing a scene with a partner. He or she will rarely refuse. When your proposal is accepted, set a date to return, sometime within the next three to five days. If it's any sooner, you probably won't be adequately prepared; any later, and you're flirting with one of the cruel realities of this business: the agent may forget you.

Once your date is set, pick a friend or an acquaintance from an acting class with whom you have a good chemistry—someone who you're comfortable with and who's strong. A good way to determine strength is to ask yourself whether the person is convincing. Acting is a collaborative partnership. If one partner is weak, the other will have to pick up the slack. If you have to do too much of that, the whole enterprise will flop.

Both the length and the subject matter of your script are crucial to your success. You don't want to bore the agent, so keep it relatively short. Around three pages is ideal. (That's about three minutes in length.) If you go over three and a half pages or four, you're inviting yawns.

Don't pick any old classic or theatrical scene. What you want is fresh, contemporary dialogue. Because it's the type of material that your agent will be sending you out for, you'll want to demonstrate your ability to handle it. The best material comes from a good acting workshop. Quite often, the instructor has scenes just obscure enough for the agent not to be familiar with them. One of the last things you want is to do a well-known scene from a movie that just about everybody's seen. You don't need the agent picturing the original stars in his or her head while you're doing the scene. Visualizing those celebrity performers, the agent will more than likely make a subconscious comparison, one that's hardly helpful.

If you wish to score the most points, you need to aim for what are, in fact, two goals in one. Firstly, you need to display your talent in a strong and convincing way—that is, as passionately and as naturally as possible. Secondly, you need to genuinely amuse or entertain the agent. If you can get him or her to smile—or better yet, laugh— you'll have that person closer to saying yes.

Obviously, you don't want to do material that's really depressing or gratuitously shocking. Avoid vulgarity, which might, under the circumstances, be considered in poor taste. Characters may indeed curse in numerous scenes, but you're not about to do a take on camera. A well-placed "damn" or "hell" here or there is acceptable, but if you use anything stronger, you run the risk of turning the agent off completely.

All things considered, you may want to try using a sitcom scene. One with a scrappy quarrel lets you display more of your emotional range. In addition, the occasional humorous barb in the middle of an altercation is entertaining. Just don't play or telegraph the humor by smiling right before the gag line is delivered. And don't forget to change the characters' names so there's no celebrity association.

In acting, as in every art, there is a constant reaching for another depth.

SIDNEY POITIER

STRATEGY NO.

93

Be Aware of the 80/20 Rule of Drama

TV and film audiences need occasional breaks from story tension. They'd feel battered all the time if the only things they ever watched were never-ending arguments or ceaseless fights.

The time between these periods of high drama is where writers use character development and expository dialogue to keep the film or series worth watching. Compared to the wilder action, moments like these feel like an emotional time-out.

If you compare the time allotted to each kind of period in a script, you'll discover that an 80/20 rule emerges. Eighty percent of a script consists of the "time-out" periods, while 20 percent is allotted to conflict or action. This is a general rule that you can depend on in all genres except action films, where the ratio is nearly reversed. However, your chances of reading for an action film are as few as the number produced in a given year. You'll encounter the other, standard stories more often.

For you, this simply means that 80 percent of all the dialogue you'll come upon will just be normal, everyday conversation. Attempting to show your stuff in an audition by melodramatically amplifying these mundane lines can be fatal. It makes you look like you're trying too hard or, worse, puts you over the top. If, on the other hand, you know you've got the sensational, conflict-ridden type of scene that makes up the other 20 percent, you can really cut loose and have fun.

The 80/20 rule even extends to the number of times you'll have each type of scene for a reading. Eighty percent can also be expressed as a ratio of four to five. This means that, on average, you can count on four out of five of your series or film auditions to contain the ordinary, conversational-type dialogue.

The 20 percent—the high drama—can be expressed as a ratio of one to five. Accordingly, you can count on one out of five auditions having this high-octane conflict. Just remember, these are averages. Make sure you know which kind of dialogue you're dealing with.

STRATEGY NO.

94

Give Splendid Speeches

Once in a while, you'll have to audition from a script that has long speeches for your character. That's six, seven, or even more nonstop lines of dialogue. As most actors will agree, this kind of reading certainly isn't easy. For one thing, it doesn't take much to lose your place while cold-reading. For another, meandering through an enormously long string of sentences can cause your performance energy to drop precipitously. A few techniques will help you convert these common drawbacks into uncommon opportunities.

Bear in mind that a character's speech is simply made up of several sentences. A sentence is nothing more than the expression of a single idea. A period indicates when one idea has ended and another one, following the period, is beginning.

Because a string of sentences is basically a succession of separate ideas, the points between them—the periods—provide excellent rest stops. In order to prevent any meandering or speeding up of your reading, just allow yourself a brief pause at the rest stops. In the real world, people occasionally pause to gather their thoughts prior to expressing them anyway. So taking a pause at these points is a natural-looking way to avoid sounding rote.

When you read through a long batch of words, deliberately pausing at the end of every, or every other, period, you can use these breaks for something else as well. You can also check in and reckon with the person reading opposite you. Looking for signs in their face or eyes that indicate whether they're being affected by your words allows you to gauge the effectiveness of your objective and whether to redouble your efforts if necessary.

Another way to gain an advantage with lengthy dialogue is to treat your character's speech as a mini-monologue. You can break up the monologue into groupings by drawing slash lines between closely related ideas and the other ideas. An example would look like this: "I want you to locate one of the passengers. She's in First Class. / I have something she needs."

The slashes provide visual anchors that assist you in relocating your lines when you return to your page after making eye contact. Also, grouping your ideas together helps focus your sense of purpose in the scene, increasing your conviction and expressiveness. (Compare Strategy no. 89.)

Use slash lines sparingly. A few help you effectively reconnect to the script as your eyes leave the page and then return to it. Too many clutter the page and defeat the purpose.

To be a good actor you have to be something like a criminal, to be willing to break the rules, to strive for something new.

NICOLAS CAGE

STRATEGY NO.

95

Stop at the Red Lights

If, during your audition, you sense your reading is going drastically awry and that you'll have no chance to pull it out of the ditch, by all means, stop. You can then ask to start over, which will help you refocus.

Don't worry about having your request turned down. Ninety-nine times out of a hundred it will be granted. Why? The people watching your audition *are on your side*. They *want* to give you the job. Life is easier for them once they've found Mr. or Ms. Right. They don't want to watch a poor performance any more than you want to give one.

STRATEGY NO.

96

Fake It till You Make It

When you have multiple pages to read with a casting director, there's often a brief lag when you turn the page and reconnect with your lines on the next page. Here's a neat little trick that will minimize that lapse, allowing you to perform with a smoother flow.

During your preparation stage, look over your scenes to see if you have the first line at the very top of any pages past page 1. If that's the case, then write it—word for word—at the bottom of the page that precedes it. Then scratch out the original typed line. Now, during the audition, when you and the casting director (or designated reader) turn the page, you will have had the last line to say. The responsibility for the next pick-up is your partner's. This not only eliminates any lull from you, but also allows you greater eye contact, keeping you alert to any unexpected changes your partner or the casting director might want to slip in at the last minute.

Live up to everybody's expectations as well as surprising them. If you're not going to be attempting to surprise the audience at the same time, well then, you're coasting.
                                                                    TOM HANKS

STRATEGY NO.

97

Own the Dialogue

Sometimes you'll encounter material in which the dialogue is poorly constructed. The wording is so stilted or stiff, it begs for some smoothing out. And if the words read that way, you'll sound that way.

If that's the case, then by all means don't hesitate to make the dialogue your own. Change a few words here and there to make it feel more comfortable. This will enable you to sound a lot more natural during your delivery. Just be careful. Owning the dialogue is a practice of making very minor changes to clumsy writing—not rewriting whole phrases.

The only situation where you should not be making any changes at all (save for an obvious typo) is in commercial auditions. The ad agencies have created phrases that are not only concise, but also legally approved and, very often, time dependent. For instance, you may have to deliver an audition that times out at precisely fifteen or thirty seconds—typical durations of commercial air time.

STRATEGY NO.

98

Watch Out for "Sort Of" and "Kind Of"

If your intent or motivation makes use of words like "sort of" or "kind of," your audition will turn out one way: underwhelming.

Vague intentions yield vague results. It's that simple. If you have an indistinct idea of what motivates your character or what you're fighting for in a scene, then the outcome will be indistinct as well. Playing "kind of displeased" or "sort of interested" guarantees you won't get the part.

Make absolutely sure you have defined your intent or action clearly and in the strongest terms conceivable long before you utter your first word in the audition.

> We're all so cloaked in unfounded opinions and unexamined information, it's a wonder we register on film at all. Absolute, nonjudgmental attentiveness is what unlocks the spirit and allows it to be seen.
>
> DEBRA WINGER

STRATEGY NO.

99

Take a Ride on the Reading

The next best thing to getting the part is being remembered. It's like money in the bank: you can pretty much rely on being called back for a later project. So be willing to risk. Stretch your neck out and be more creative at each successive audition.

Casting directors watch lots of actors playing it safe all day long. So when someone comes in and does something beyond the ordinary, they take note. So what if your choices aren't the correct ones? If they're as creative as they are convincing, you'll have secured a place in the casting director's memory.

There's only one minor exception however, to this worthwhile tactic. You can find out about it in the next Strategy.

STRATEGY NO.

100

Assess the Role Size

"Eliminate the obvious" and "play against type" are two of the recurring bits of advice actors often hear from their teachers. While those kinds of recommendations are meant to bring about memorable performances, they overlook a pivotal reality.

Directors don't normally look for memorable performances for extremely small, one- or two-line parts. In the world of TV, small parts are normally considered clichés that the TV-viewing public can readily digest. The bored waitress, the no-non-sense traffic cop, and the robotic government agent with the aviator-style glasses are just some of those persistent clichés. Consequently, you stand a better chance of nailing one of these roles if you don't try to get too cute or creative.

On the other hand, principal parts with several lines or several scenes allow for more latitude. Once you're sure you're reading for a role of this type, have fun and put your own personal stamp on it.

Communicating [in scenes] is a very brave thing to do, because you have to be open. You have to be able to listen.
JAMIE LEE CURTIS

STRATEGY NO.
101

Strive for Excellence, Not Perfection

Perfection is a seductive impostor. By holding out the promise of arriving one day at an impossible standard, it invariably breeds intolerance and self-loathing. Perfectionists may get a lot done, but where they really excel is in masking an underlying fear of failure.

Striving for excellence, on the other hand, is a distinction that fosters a healthier sense of self-regard. By accepting occasional mistakes as an essential part of the road to growth and accomplishment, you feel better, perform better, and, almost daily, reaffirm faith in your own potential. Live out your life standing in this distinction, and you can't help but build a secure foundation for a winning attitude—the most indispensable Strategy of them all.

Whatever you want to do, do it now! There are only so many tomorrows.

MICHAEL LANDON

SELECTED BIBLIOGRAPHY

Adams, Brian. *Screen Acting.* Los Angeles: Lone Eagle, 1992.

Blanchard, Nina. *How to Break into Motion Pictures, Television, Commercials and Modeling.* Garden City, NY: Doubleday, 1978.

Cohen, Alan. *I Had It All the Time.* Port Huron, MI: RLS Associates, 1995.

Henry and Rogers. *How to Be a Working Actor.* New York: Backstage Books, 1994.

Park, Lawrence. *Acting Truths and Fictions.* Hollywood, CA: Acting World Books, 1995.

Sonenberg, Jane. *The Actor Speaks: Twenty-four Actors Talk about Process and Technique.* New York: Crown, 1996.